PREACHER
in a
HARD HAT

PREACHER
in a
HARD HAT

A Guide to Preaching
for PASTORS and EVERYONE ELSE

JIM SCHMITMEYER

CHALICE
PRESS

ST. LOUIS, MISSOURI

Bible quotations, unless otherwise noted, are from the *New Revised Standard Version Bible*, copyright 1989, Division of Christian Education of the National Council of the Churches of Christ in the United States of America. Used by permission. All rights reserved.

Cover photo: Getty Images
Cover and interior design: Elizabeth Wright

Visit Chalice Press on the World Wide Web at
www.chalicepress.com

10 9 8 7 6 5 4 3 2 1   06 07 08 09 10

Library of Congress Cataloging-in-Publication Data
Schmitmeyer, James M.
  Preacher in a hard hat : a guide to preaching for pastors and everyone else / Jim Schmitmeyer.
    p. cm.
  ISBN-13: 978-0-8272-2985-3 (pbk.)
  ISBN-10: 0-8272-2985-2 (pbk.)
  1. Catholic preaching. 2. Catholic Church—Sermons. 3. Sermons, American—21st century. I. Title.
  BX1795.P72S36 2006
  251—dc22
                                                    2005037795

Printed in the United States of America

To the People of St. Al's

Contents

Acknowledgments

I wish to thank my agent, Les Stobbe and my personal editor, Laura Chamberlain. I also wish to express gratitude for the many friends and parishioners who assisted and supported me in the writing of this book.

PART 1

Goals and Strategies of Homiletic Preaching

CHAPTER 1

Schmoe's Auto Body

The church echoed with the sound of hammers and drills. Workers scurried about, shouted from ladders, and shoved pews across the floor.

A flurry of activity—from carpet installment to door hanging to fire department inspection—heralded the soon-to-be-completed renovation of St. Aloysius Church. I fell in step with Steve Hudepohl, the project manager. Our destination: a stack of wooden crates piled askew on the choir platform.

It was four days before Christmas and two day before the rededication. Time was tight and tempers were short. Just that morning, the music director confronted me: "A dedication ceremony? Two days before Christmas? Father, what were we thinking?"

But I was excited. Steve's crew had done an excellent job keeping the project on schedule. I had marveled at his ability to coordinate workers from various trades. Some had worked through the night just to maintain the momentum.

For three months, the parish had celebrated Sunday worship in the school gymnasium. It was time to return to Jerusalem. The gates of the temple beckoned.

3

You bet I was excited.

Steve and I reached the crates. Inside awaited thirty-six organ pipes, the centerpiece of the renovation project.

Steve took the pry bar to the first crate. The lid creaked open. And I choked.

There was a word in my throat that I couldn't say in church.

"They're tin!" I looked at Steve in disbelief. "They're galvanized tin!"

"Aren't they supposed to be gold?" Steve was already prying open a second crate.

Soon the lids were off. And the pipes were exposed in all their utilitarian starkness.

I shook my head. "They look like furnace ducts."

Steve put down the bar and shoved back his hard hat. "They don't exactly match the décor."

We checked the purchase order and contacted the organ company. The company had made a mistake. Two painters were dispatched to guild the pipes. If they worked through the night, they might meet the deadline.

But one problem remained: no safe place to execute the work.

I stepped outside. A cold drizzle was falling and I had no coat, but I didn't care. I hunched my shoulders, put my hands in my pockets, and sulked down the street. The world was gray. I heard a siren in the distance and rounded the corner. The bent grills on the wrecked cars at Schmoe's Auto Body sneered as I walked by.

One of the shop doors clanked opened. "What's the good word, Padre?"

It was Schmoe.

I shuffled inside and told him my woes. He wiped thinner from his hand. "We've got two paint rooms here. You can have them both."

You can't beat having neighbors like this.

According to the Bible, thirty thousand lumberjacks, seventy thousand transporters, and eighty thousand stonecutters contributed to the building of Solomon's Temple. It doesn't mention auto body workers. But for a certain congregation in suburban Cincinnati, the boys at Schmoe's saved the day. Their example, and that of every worker who has ever labored behind the scenes, reminds us that things such as organs and harps, vestments and hymnals form but one facet of the worship of God.

Blueprints, paint fumes, and callused hands also render glory to the Lord of life.

This book is intended to help the people of God—preachers and listeners alike—make vital connections between the lunchrooms at work and the altars in our churches, textbooks on school desks and Bibles on nightstands, the washing of one's car and the cleansing of one's soul. Herein lies an invitation for everyone involved in preaching—the speaking, the listening, the studying, the shaping of God's Word for Sunday worship—to coordinate their efforts and focus their energies.

Just as the building of a church requires a host of trades—from architects to supervisors to electricians—the preaching of God's work is a group effort. Why? Because the Word of God is not confined to texts written in Hebrew and Greek; it involves more than the arduous study of a pastor laboring over various translations and biblical commentaries. The Word is a living reality. As John puts it, "What was from the beginning, what we have heard, what we have seen with our eyes, what we have looked at and touched with our hands...concern[s] the word of life." (1 Jn. 1:1)

Within the body of Christ, hearing and speaking the Word of God entails mutual inspiration between preachers and listeners. This back-and-forth influence is evident not only when pastors deliver their sermons from the pulpit but also in the work that precedes the final product. Clearly, preaching involves living realities as well as ancient ones.

If you believe that pastors and parishioners have valuable insights to offer one another in the hearing of the Word and the shaping of the homily, this book is for you.

Sunday Chimes, Daily Grind

I love Sundays: the music, the fellowship, light beams streaming through the stained glass. There is excitement in the air, a sense of anticipation among the people. Candles are lit; the fragrance of incense hints at the mysteries soon to unfold.

But from where I sit, the view isn't always sunny. As a pastor of a church where 1,700 people gather to worship each weekend, I observe a host of expressions on the faces of my congregants.

I spot Rick, a young husband whose brow remains furrowed despite the lilting strains of a hymn of praise. His preoccupation, I suspect, centers on the expiration of his unemployment benefits and the upcoming birth of his second child.

A few pews back is Jill. She's a nurse on the night shift. Her husband is a long-distance trucker. Her son is rebellious.

She yawns.

I notice David and Clara, a retired couple with lovely smiles and gracious manners. Only their closest friends and I know that a grandson addicted to drugs recently ransacked their apartment.

Throughout the opening rites, I gaze upon the flock that has been entrusted to my care. I long to preach to them a word of healing, comfort, clarity, and direction. I have studied the sacred texts and probed their historical, social, and political contexts. I have taken the holy words into the quiet of my prayer. Yet my urgent hope is that the homily I deliver will transform words about shepherds and centurions into a message pertinent to commuters, producers, and consumers. My goal is to construct a bridge sturdy enough to transport my listeners from marketplaces where sparrows were sold for two pennies to a world of variable interest rates, Wal-Mart parking lots, and eBay auctions.

I am sorely aware that biblical commentaries and translations go only so far.

How might Jill, whose son is uncontrollable, respond to the psalm that sings of a soul resting in the Creator's lap like a child on a mother's knee (Ps. 131:2)?

Will Rick's self-doubt be further eroded by Paul's axiom, "Those who do not work should not eat" (2 Thess. 3:10, author's trans.)?

What encouragement can a couple in David and Clara's situation possibly draw from the story of the prodigal son?

Martin Luther once quipped that had he realized what preaching would entail, he would not have allowed twenty-four horses to drag him into a pulpit.

No doubt about it, preaching is a challenging and difficult task.

As a Catholic priest schooled in the field of homiletics, I have occasionally found myself envious of the fact that my Protestant colleagues refer to their places of work as "a study." At a Catholic parish, pastors refer to their workspace as "an office." One word connotes an atmosphere of reflection and prayer; the latter conjures up images of file cabinets, appointment books, staff memos, finance reports, and missives from diocesan headquarters...all with phones and doorbells ringing in the background.

Of course, generalizations are misleading. Truth be told, neither designation, "study" nor "office," manages to capture the necessity of moving to another venue to conduct essential tasks in preparing the Sunday sermon. What is the proper name of the place where God's Word waits to be engaged in depth?

It's called "the field."

Members of churches with full-time clergy, who provide their pastors with an office or a study, take a risk with the ministry of preaching. Full-time pastors will be less likely to include in their preaching an echo of assembly-line tedium or the temptation of lunchroom gossip, just as congregations with celibate clergy seldom hear references to piles of laundry or infants with colic.

The fact of the matter is that no single preacher—male or female, married or unmarried, young or old—can ever fully enter into the life experience of a congregation. Still, the goal of the Sunday message remains the same: to make connections between the world of the listeners and the Word of God. Because both spheres are infinitely complex, consultation between preacher and listener is of infinite help.

Can you imagine Jesus preaching to roughneck fishermen without ever stepping into a skiff? It's a bit like trying to imagine a news reporter passing up the chance to interview a lottery winner. Yet church-goers can quickly call to mind a preacher "without a clue" when it comes to "real life."

What to do? Just beyond the door of the pastor's study or office lie the job sites, classrooms, family rooms, truck stops, conference rooms, playgrounds, gyms, and cafeterias where most of our listeners spend a lot of their time. If you're a pastor, make yourself available. If you're a parishioner, invite your pastor to work.

Fortunately, pastors and laity alike have the example of the Master, who shows us that a preacher's words must be *drawn from life* in order to *give life.*

From Deskwork to Fieldwork

Certain events occur in an individual's life that leave a mark on that person's character. For me, a vivid memory often returns during those opening rites of the liturgy as I gaze upon the faces of those waiting to hear the Word of God.

It is a sunny morning on the grounds of a seminary where I am taking a walk with some fellow students. A new school year has just begun, and the trees are beginning to take on the colors of autumn. The air is sharp with light, and I am not particularly engaged in the conversation of my companions.

The time for lunch draws near, and we turn a corner past the maintenance shop where one of the groundskeepers has a tractor up on blocks. As we walk by, the worker scoots from beneath the chassis and gives a nod. We exchange greetings, but once out of earshot, one of my companions turns, holds up his hands, and makes an incredibly arrogant remark: "Brothers, these hands were made for chalices, not calluses."

The anger that remark provoked remains with me to this day. Fortunately, God has allowed me to channel the energy of that emotion to fuel a holy drive: to be as connected to my parishioners as possible...so that my preaching might be as effective as possible.

The parish that I serve is not significantly different than other suburban churches. Nor is the compassion I feel for my flock notably different from that of any other dedicated pastor. But there are unique dimensions to how my parish engages the Word of God. At St. Al's, my parishioners and I are committed to ongoing discussions and investigations into God's Word that place the connections between scripture and daily life front and center in the homiletic process. Of course, our endeavors are limited, and the results are sometimes lacking. But after four years of effort, the work of directly involving parishioners in the homiletic task is yielding noticeable results.

But first, some background.

When I arrived at St. Aloysius Parish in Bridgetown, a blue-collar suburb of Cincinnati, I had served two rural communities for more than a decade. In contrast to quiet villages of thirty houses each, my new parish comprised fifteen hundred households and a K-8 parochial school.

It was not my idea to come to the suburbs. While serving in the country, I had become deeply involved in agricultural issues affecting the economies and social structure of my communities. I reveled in "hands-on" aspects of being a rural pastor. Because I was raised on a dairy farm, I had enough competence to help my parishioners with barn chores and fieldwork, especially at those times when someone fell ill or was a victim of a farming accident.

The experience of shepherding a rural community was incredibly fulfilling for me—physically, emotionally, and spiritually. I had been raised on the axiom, "If you're close to the soil, you're close to God." So for this pastor, the connections between God, community, worship, and scripture were as obvious as sunlight in July.

The shift to suburban ministry was unsettling, to say the least.

The Quakers have a saying, "God will make a way." I am glad to report that it applies to non-Quakers as well. My new community in Bridgetown, on the outskirts of Cincinnati, turned out to be wonderfully friendly and welcoming. At first the site of my horse trailer parked behind the rectory seemed a bit odd to them. But once they learned to know me, they didn't seem to mind having a pastor who drove a pickup with a dog in the bed of the truck. If nothing else, it gave them something to smile about.

But for me, a common language had been lost. Gone was the banter with altar servers about 4–H club projects or county fairs. Conversations with adults no longer concerned the farm market report or the amount of rainfall.

Rather, it was soccer, volleyball, and computer games that occupied the youngsters' free time. And it was traffic bulletins, not weather reports, that determined the climate at the start of the suburban day.

All this was to be expected. But there was one aspect of suburban life that caught me off guard. In my initial months at St. Al's, I noticed that, without my prodding, no one ever mentioned his or her job or career.

I experienced the lack of this knowledge as a gaping absence in my preaching. I recall trying not to employ agrarian illustrations in my homilies, though sometimes I did revert to some agricultural example. My new parishioners expressed appreciation for the insights. I thanked them for the comments. But inwardly I knew that the effect of my preaching was far from illuminating. It was merely quaint.

Take Your Pastor to Work

Given the initial discomfort I experienced in my new pastoral setting, I decided to address my lack of knowledge regarding the social context of my parish in a couple of ways. First, I urged parishioners to consider hosting homily reflection groups in their homes that I would attend with notepad in hand. Second, to capture something of a feel for the places where they spent most of their time, I initiated a "take your pastor to work" program, extending an offer to accompany those interested in giving me a tour of their workplaces or job sites, join them for lunch in the break room, or, if possible, shadow them as they carried out their tasks.

At a later point, the parish Web site was redesigned to include a form for parishioners to submit homily input and feedback.

These attempts to better connect the Word of God with the day-to-day lives of my parishioners were worth the effort. The chapters ahead will explore the manner and ways in which these efforts bore fruit.

Summary

The heart of liturgical preaching is making accessible to contemporary believers the life-force of God encoded in the scriptures as well as the liturgy, teaching, and life of the church. The primary goal of this chapter was to convince preachers and listeners that the homiletic process is enriched when they join together in reflecting on the scriptures before Sunday worship.

A second goal was to encourage pastors to extend the scope of their homily preparation from *textual* study to include direct, *contextual* analysis.

The third goal was to invite the listeners of the Sunday homily to recognize the value of their input in the pastor's work of discerning the meaning of God's Word within the setting of their parish.

In the sample homily that follows, the results of the pastor's deskwork is found in the opening section, where the historical and political dimension of the gospel text are framed in contemporary terms. The illustrations in the body of the homily were drawn from a discussion between the preacher and a homily reflection group.

HOMILY: The Badlands of Advent

Text: Luke 3:1–18
Occasion: Second Sunday of Advent, Year C

In the fifteenth year of the reign of Emperor Tiberius,
when Philip was tetrarch and Pilate was governor...

Well, who cares?
Seriously, does anyone here care
who governed the region at the time of John of the Baptist?
Or who the tetrarch was? Or the emperor, for that matter?

Granted, from the standpoint of history,
the information is important.

But who cares?
That's precisely the point, you see.
No one cares!

The presumptuous tone that colors this verse
is a joke worthy of Jay Leno or Dave Letterman,
and Luke's gospel uses it to full effect:

Who *cares* about the pomp of earthly rulers
when God's own Messiah,
the Savior of the world,
is born in a rickety shack for livestock?
The rulers are about to be taken by surprise
by a carpenter waiting in line to be baptized
in a muddy river somewhere out in the wilderness.

Welcome to the badlands, folks!
A place where the arrogant are mocked.
A place where rocks jab the soles of the feet of people
who are fed up with
the corruption in their clergy,
the oppression of their rulers,
and the sin in their own lives.

It's where the wilderness and the landscape isn't pretty.

If it were a Hollywood movie,
the scene would be a wasteland
smoldering in the aftermath of an intergalactic war,
a place of ominous shadows and ruined settlements,
a place where children beg
and twisted shells of armored vehicles litter the roadsides,
a society in tatters, a populace buffeted by storms of
    brutality.

Welcome to the badlands of the Bible.

You know the scene. You know its feel.

There, amid the blowing sand, John lifts a man from the
    river.
And we watch in silence
as water washes dust from the face of the Hero
sent to rescue humanity.
We see him regain his footing, shake back his hair.
A man with eyes as piercing as the light of the desert sun.
A man with a plan as sharp as the rocks that cut his feet.

And so it begins.
The first luminous mystery.
The beginning of Jesus' ministry.

It takes shape on the frontier.
It begins in the badlands.

So, what does this have to do with people like us
in a nice suburb called Bridgetown, Ohio?

Well, let me tell you about a teenager named April.
She's a member of our parish.
A girl with a good family who attends a good school
and who lives in a nice neighborhood.
But come summer, she's going to the badlands.
She's been there before and can't wait to get back.

She's not following her friends to the beaches of Florida.
She's headed instead to the sandy border between Mexico
    and Texas;
to a run-down day-care center
where the eyes of the children of the poor
sparkle in the light of the same sun
that glistened on the water of the River Jordan.

Jesus' ministry was in the badlands.
So too is April's.

Though it varies with each individual,
there's a distinct pattern in the way that God draws us to
    himself.
At some point or another our journey is going to take us
    through some broken land.

From the day that Abraham and Sarah packed up their
    belongings
and began their trek to the Promised Land with a portable
    tent…
to the day that Naomi and Ruth clung to each other
on the windswept border between Judah and Moab…
to that night when Joseph adjusted the packs on the donkey
that would carry Mary and the Infant to safety in Egypt…

"All God's people," as the old spiritual put it,
"need travelin' shoes."

Sometimes the broken land, the desert land,
is closer than we know.

There's a contractor from our parish
who recently told me about stumbling into such a place
    some years ago.

It happened when he stopped by the apartment
of some new workers on his construction crew.

"These fellows," he told me, "Jose and Manuel.
They're among the best workers I got and I pay them well.
But they use candles instead of lamps. They don't have a TV.
They won't pay a dime for the extra electricity…
or anything else they don't think they need."
He shook his head.
"It's amazing. All their money goes back home."

I looked at him. "You admire them, don't you?"

"Yes, I do."
He crossed his arms and leaned on the fender of his truck.
"You know, I'm glad God lets my small company
make some difference in this messed up world."

A voice cries out in the desert,
"Make straight the way of the Lord."

Welcome to the badlands.

CHAPTER 2

Greg's Bass Boat

The hour is early, and the group is small. But the coffee is great; Walt brews it.

Walt also sends advance notice of meetings, assigns discussion leaders, decides topics for study, provides worksheets to fill out, and makes certain the meetings end on time.

This particular morning, Fred, a new member of the parish, strolls into the room fifteen minutes after the meeting begins. It's his first time, and he apologizes for being late.

He is welcomed by all present, and Walt resumes leading the discussion. The topic: anger management.

"So, Jesus knocked over the tables, right? Question one in the workbook: How can Jesus' anger in Matthew 21:12–13 be reconciled with his teaching in Matthew 5:22?"

"Ah, yes." Fred gets settled at the table. "A key verse. Given by God, I'm convinced, for the purpose of self-knowledge: 'If you are angry with a brother…you will be liable to judgment.'"

Tony stirs his coffee. "I'd say you really know your Bible, Fred."

"I grew up Baptist."

Walt clears his voice. "Well, we all know in this case that Jesus had good reason to be angry." He flips a page in the workbook.

"Question two: When is anger appropriate?" His eyes scan the faces. "Greg?"

"If I may break in." Fred looks upward and squints. "I assume all of you are aware that the book of Exodus describes God's wrath in detail." He opens his Bible. "If I could read…"

Greg gets up. "Anyone need coffee?"

Tony hands Greg his cup. "My wife's got a bit of a temper. Janice ever get on your case, Greg?"

Greg laughs. "Why do you think I spend so much time fishing?"

Tony shakes his head. "You got more patience than me." He turns to Fred."Greg's good at hooking bass."

Fred smiles. "I'd never have the patience to be a fisherman, gentlemen. But speaking of patience, it does appear that God occasionally loses his. For example," he adjusts his glasses, "There's this blunt warning given to the Israelites in Numbers 12:9."

Greg scratches his head. "Isn't there a verse where Jesus says, 'I will make you bass fishermen?'"

"Fred," Walt's voice is bit louder than it needs to be. "You're going a bit deep for us. We got this workbook, see?"

"I'm sorry, Walt, continue. I just want to say that I think this Bible study is just what our parish needs."

Walt lets out a sigh. "Question three: What makes you angry? Silence.

"Greg?"

Greg frowns.

"Tony?"

"My mother-in-law just moved in. Where do you want me to start?"

Laughter.

"Now, gentlemen." Fred closes his Bible, taps his finger on the cover. "God has set his plan in place before us…"

Walter throws up his hands. "It's half past the hour and we got eight questions to go!"

"Easy, Walt." Greg's voice is steady. "There's room in my boat. What do you say we leave at ten?"

———

You get the point. Spiritual meetings are not immune to rough edges. Homiletic listening—the practice of straining to hear the heartbeat of the parish in diverse situations—often means listening past rough edges and around sharp corners.

This chapter is about listening.

Listening through the Emotion

Friends, and pastors who dare to be friends, are usually aware of personal issues that give rise to the hesitations and tremors heard in the voices of those they know well. In the case of the men's Bible study, for instance, Walt's high need for order belies a past history of addiction. Fred's intellectual posturing exposes insecurities of another sort.

As a priest, I have learned that the penitential screen is no shield for disguising the subtle gasps and sighs of the soul. Any sensitive pastor soon learns to detect the distress signals that show up in marriage counseling, youth retreats, performance appraisals, and even at the door of the church on bright, sunny mornings.

Awareness of the emotion in the voices of one's friends and fellow parishioners will lead the attentive reader of scripture to note similar signals in biblical personages. It won't matter if the Bible reflection occurs in a group setting or in private prayer; a person with an ear tuned for emotion will discover hints of joy, anxiety, relief, sadness, and other myriad facets of feeling throughout the Bible. Consider the following verses:

"The moment your greeting reached my ears…!"

"We have no food to give them."

"Lord, if you had been here…"

"You still do not know me, Philip?"

"You will not wash my feet!"

"Where have you laid him?"

Occasionally, a lector at Mass will capture the undulating manner in which such words and phrases sweep across the terrain of a soul. The skill of such readers will open the way for listeners to take note in the way that a young child hears a message of praise in an upward lift of the parent's voice or the way an elderly person strolling through a park enjoys the sound of leaves swirling in a whirlwind.

The movement of the Spirit lies within the sound of the words and awaits release through the flow of the phrases.

When a reader engages the Word in the company of friends, verses with hints of emotion are sometimes repeated; read a second time with different tones and shades of meaning applied. This in turn elicits multiple insights as the group members consider various levels of meaning.

Someone says, "That's interesting—the attitude, I mean. That woman at the well was…gutsy."

Another person adds, "I can see her with a hand on hip, her nose in the air."

Statements like these serve as entry points into experience-oriented perspectives. Like doors left ajar, they throw light into unexplored rooms, inviting discussion of dimensions of faith that are otherwise left in the shadows.

Listening through the Noise

The guitar squeals are so piercing that you can't hear the pounding of your own fists on the door. "I said, *Turn it down! Now!*"

The memory of the confrontation returns as soon as your hand slams the snooze alarm. Out in the kitchen the TV is tuned to CNN. You hear the sound of water running. The dog barks. Your husband is trying to sing in the shower. A computer game beeps and pops. A commercial screams out used car values. The dog keeps barking. Your six-year-old stands at the door, "Mom, my belly…" You fall back on your pillow; there's a ringing in your ear. The alarm squawks again. You get up. You're late. You rehearse excuses for the boss.

It's just another morning. No time for scripture, prayer, or praise. A kiss at the door. Coffee gulped then spilled in the car. You turn on the radio, turn at the light, ease onto the tollway, then grip the wheel as the howl of a semi approaches from behind.

It's just another morning.

What light can the Word of God shed on mornings like this? Does the high level of noise that we encounter in our world thoroughly drown out any whisper of grace?

If we listen carefully, we'll hear some noise and realize that not all is a peaceful silent night.

Read almost any verse, and it is possible to supply the missing background sounds. In Bible days ox carts creaked and drovers yelled and snapped their whips. The drones of men at prayer wafted through the windows of synagogues. Hatchets hacked. Chisels chinked. Birds sang. Babies cried. In the market vendors shouted and buyers bargained.

Consider all that took place along the road that Jesus traveled to Jerusalem: People whooped and shouted, hollered and clapped. Demons screamed. Debates raged, and words shot like arrows through the air. Demonstrations. Recriminations. Denunciations. Then came the sound of swords and lanterns snaking up the path on the Mount of Olivet. Pilate's sneer. The howl of the mob. Armor clanking. Soldiers hissing.

Enter the *Via Dolorosa* and witness the unfolding of the Sorrowful Mysteries.

The slap of reeds, the zing of whips. Jeers and taunts. Hammers striking nails. Thunder in a blackened sky.

The Bible is far from silent. Indeed, the great act of our salvation comes wrapped in a cacophony of hatred and confusion.

In light of this, the noise of our lives seems more manageable, but what meaning might it hold? Might we discern within the rush of our lives the vague outlines of Christ's timeless mission, of which we are a part?

It's a worthwhile question, and when parishioners and pastors join together to reflect on the Word of God, they are in a position to assist one another in listening through the noise of the world and recall Christ's challenge to his followers to be *in the world* but not *of the world.*

So, how do we go about listening through the noise?

The process is different from listening through emotion because, in the rush of life, there exists minimal time for analysis. Like a point guard on the basketball court, information rushes in. Tension builds. Muscles tense. We pivot, we fake, we break. Somehow, in the midst of the chaos, we recall the drills, engage our talent, test our skill.

And strain to hear the voice of the Coach.

Clearly, there are times when we need to muster the determination of an athlete who "plays through the pain."

This, too, is prayer. In the press of a competitive world, even our hectic lives and frantic efforts give honor and praise to God. The following passage from the book of Sirach captures the spiritual value intrinsic to human work.

> So with the smith standing near his anvil,
>   forging crude iron.
> The heat of the fire sears his flesh,
>   yet he toils away in the furnace heat.
> The clang of the hammer deafens his ears,
>   his eyes are fixed on the tool he is shaping.
> His care is to finish his work,
>   and he keeps watch till he perfects it in detail.
> So with the potter sitting at his labor,
>   revolving the wheel with his feet.

He is always concerned for his products
    and turns them out in quantity.
With his hands he molds the clay,
    and with his feet he softens it.
His care is for proper coloring,
    and he keeps watch on the fire in his kiln.

Without them no city could be lived in…
they maintain God's ancient handiwork.
           (Sir. 38:28–32a; 34a, author's translation)

A foundry worker sits in my office. We are chatting. He describes the danger and physical toil involved in his work. He also mentions the hard drinking and failed marriages of many of his coworkers.

"Is it hard to be a man of faith in that world?" I ask.

Before he speaks, his eyes tell the answer.

"It's rough," he says. "But God gave me a wonderful wife." His voice trails off. "And my family?" He frowns, looks down at his hands. "I'd die for them."

Conversations like this illustrate that preaching is more a matter of listening than speaking. If pastors and parishioners have ears to hear, the promises of Christ permeate the ruckus of a household at the beginning of the day, and the clatter of iron on a factory floor echoes the sound of hammers striking nails on Calvary.

Listening through the Scriptures

This chapter opened with a replay of a men's Bible study. The interaction between Walt, Fred, Tony, and Greg demonstrates how discussions of the Bible can easily fracture along lines of differing expectations.

Some Bible study groups focus on theology; some function as spiritual support groups; still others offer a blend of the two. A homily reflection group, on the other hand, has a distinct purpose and a unique character.

What unfolds during a meeting of a homily reflection group?

When parishioners are unaccustomed to homiletic reflections, they often arrive at the sessions feeling insecure about what they have to offer. It is usually expressed in self-effacing phrases like, "I'm not too familiar with the Bible, Father," or "I'm not sure what I'm doing here, but I figured there'd be refreshments."

The need for clarity of purpose is obvious. A brief discussion about the human longing to be in touch with God is an effective way to begin. I often mention that, just as I need to study the *texts* of the Sunday scriptures, I also need to know the *contexts* in which those scriptures are to be lived. This assures the participants that they do indeed have valuable insights to contribute to the preaching process.

I then ask them to think about how the words of the homily can best address their spiritual needs. Seldom do they indicate a need for specific information or some sort of instruction about the faith. They openly acknowledge what all worshipers desire: a deeper awareness of the presence of God.

Indeed, the reason we Christians gather for worship is to enter into a deeper experience of the presence of Christ. Because preaching is a central part of our experience of worship, its main purpose is not to instruct Christians in the content of their faith, but to *deepen their recognition* of the presence of Christ in their midst.

From this perspective, the role of the homily reflection group makes eminent sense: With a passage of scripture as a field of reference, the participants seek to identify moments of grace in ordinary life in order to inform the experience of the Word and deepen the praise of the community come Sunday morning.

During a discussion, a volunteer is asked to read one of the scriptural passages for the upcoming Sunday. If the passage is intricate, we may ask the volunteer to read it several times. Occasionally, we'll want to hear the passage read by several different readers in order to catch various nuances within the words and phrases. Once the passage has been read and sufficiently heard, the members are invited to share whatever images, memories, or questions that a particular word or phrase may have elicited in their minds.

Often, this part of the session elicits some degree of confusion. Sometimes it is reminiscent of the passage about the two disciples making their way to Emmaus following the crucifixion, unaware of the resurrection. You may recall their consternation as they attempted to insert the Word of God into the muddle of current events.

Their hopes had been dashed and their expectations unfulfilled. It was not easy for Cleopas and his companion to connect the words of scripture with their immediate experience. Nor is it for us today. After all, the words are ancient, sometimes archaic. Furthermore, when our own dreams go unfulfilled, we find ourselves falling in alongside the disciples trudging toward Emmaus: our feet drag in the dust; God is a stranger; and we're left trying to figuring things out on our own.

But at this point, the group has engaged a particular passage, and the process will likely unfold according to the pattern of the story of the road to Emmaus: The words and verses seem to crunch like gravel beneath our feet:

"That phrase makes me think of a time when…";

"That comment reminds me of something my sixteen-year-old said…";

"I get mad at God when things don't go my way";

"When I hear about healings, I wonder why my nephew had to die."

And so the discussion unfolds. We share concerns, tell of joys, renew our hope. At times, we shake our heads in sorrow. Occasionally, we stumble in our efforts to express our faith and discover that leaning on one another is the only way we can continue.

"The Stones Will Shout."

Do not fear the dismay. At certain points in the walk through a passage, some members of the group may want to stop, insisting that "an answer" be applied to a question that has emerged. Yet, as recorded in the journey to Emmaus, not even the answers supplied by the Risen Lord truly satisfied the anxiety of Cleopas and his friend. It was not until the two of them invited the mysterious Stranger to dine with them that their eyes were opened.

This point is essential to note: the reliability of Christ's explanation of the scriptures only sank in *after they recognized his presence* at the table. The key to fruitful homiletic reflection is happening upon moments of grace where the presence of Christ is somehow revealed in the midst of our day-to-day life. It is then that we realize how deeply the words of his teaching burn in our hearts.

At this point, someone needs to reach down and retrieve from among the pebbles on the path a smooth, flat stone, the kind that children love to skip across the service of a stream or pond:

"Saint Paul is talking about finishing the race. Let me tell you this, when our boy Justin crossed the line and won his event at the Special Olympics, well, I can't tell you how proud I was."

"Nicodemus wonders how a person can be reborn?

Obviously, he never suffered clinical depression."

"Forty years in the desert? Wondering whether you'd have food in the morning? That reminds me of the year I was laid off. I learned a lot about trust. But it didn't come easy."

As the stone skims the surface, ripples of grace spread out, and evidence of God's presence begins to emerge from the interface between contemporary life and the ancient words. Through such mutual sharing in faith, the Word takes on flesh, and Christ's church is moved to praise.

Summary

Whenever the preacher is privileged to witness the movement of God's Spirit within the life of the community or take part in a group discussion on the work of God in their midst, there may be examples that so closely align themselves to the spirit of the passage that the preacher may wish to ask permission to incorporate the reference into the Sunday homily. Such permission is necessary. But for the pastor, it is the gleaning of insight, not homily illustrations, that serves as the primary benefit of a homily reflection group.

HOMILY:
Leaving Parents, Fishing Nets, and Lawnmowers Behind
Text: Matthew 4:12–23
Occasion: Third Sunday in Ordinary Time

Recently, a grandfather in our parish
was helping his grandson with his religion homework.
The boy is going to be confirmed in a couple of weeks,
and the catechism lesson
focused on the story we just heard
about James and John,
dropping their smelly fishing nets
at the feet of their old man, Zebedee,
then traipsing off after Jesus
without a second thought.

Without so much as a

"Good-bye, Dad!"

"Good-bye, hooks and barbs!"
"Good-bye, catfish stings!"

The grandfather asks the boy,
"Could *you* just leave everything
if Jesus asked you to follow him?"

This boy's been trained well here at St. Al's.
Without hesitation, he said yes.

But his grandfather pressed him.
He knows how much this boy loves motors.
You see, the boy's dad has a lawn mower repair shop,
and his son is a chip off the old man's block.

This kid loves nothing better
than getting a lawn mower
back into working order,
especially if it's one that his dad has shoved aside
and declared "not worth the effort."

So his grandfather asked him again,
"So, you'd really leave your Mom and Dad
and never step foot in the lawn mower shop again?"

And the boy thought for a moment and said,

"Well, maybe that would be pretty hard."

And this brings up a detail of the gospel story
that goes unrecorded:
How old were James and John at the time they were called?

Were they young?

Young enough to be straining for a taste
of freedom, adventure and glory?

Or were they mature?

Mature enough to realize
that their lot in life was set.

Or maybe the gospel passage omits
recording their chronological age
for another reason.

Is this passage telling us that it doesn't matter
if you're young or old…

it doesn't matter if you're a fisher…
or a lawn mower fixer…

That there is going to be a *restlessness* inside you
that God—and only God—can satisfy?

An older translation of the Bible said,
"Man does not live on bread alone" (Deut. 8:3; Mt. 4:4).

In contemporary language that means,
"You can't live on a career alone."

A life with no meaning
is worse that a life with no income.

"No money" affects how well you eat,
but "no meaning" kills the soul.

Furthermore, sins can be forgiven,
but a loss of meaning is hard to replace.

Today's gospel passage shows us Peter and Andrew,
James and John leaving their nets and livelihoods behind,
but the point is not about abandonment of family.

The lesson is this:
A passionate life demands everything you've got.

Meaning is measured in drops of blood,
not in dollars and cents.

Do you ever wonder why
our hearts are designed as to never be satisfied?

It's because we're all made in God's image,
and in some ways,
God is like that two-year-old of yours who never sits still.
God is like the friend who keeps calling with weekend plans.
God is that kid in the repair shop who can't put the wrench
    down until the
sputtering engine coughs itself into a start.

Our souls are restless for God
because God is restless for us.

A woman in our homily reflection group this week put it
    best:
"I am so excited," she said.

"I don't know what lies ahead,
but I know God is calling me somewhere.
I don't know where.
I just pray that I recognize any sign God might give.
God's my guide, and that's all that matters."

Her words touch something deep within us all.

They awaken a memory of what it's like
to have a sense of mission,
a sense of adventure,
an awareness that attaching oneself to Christ
means being enticed…

If you're elderly, you refer to this experience as *grace;*
if you're middle aged, you might call it a *purpose-driven life;*
if you're young, you might call it *"living on the edge."*

If you're Christian, it's summed up in the words,
"Come, follow me."

CHAPTER 3

Tabitha's Quilt

Her name was Tabitha, and she was an accomplished seamstress (Acts 9:36ff). When Tabitha died, her friends and neighbors sent for the apostle Peter, who was visiting in a nearby town. Upon his arrival at Tabitha's house, he found all her friends crying. Immediately they told him about what a good woman Tabitha was and how deeply she was devoted to Christ.

Then they showed him some of the beautiful things Tabitha had sewn.

Clearly, showing Peter those garments—quilts, aprons, pillowcases, baby blankets, whatever it was that she had sewn—was important. The items represented the life of someone they loved; they were physical objects Peter could see. Most of all, the fine cloth and quality stitching gave Tabitha's friends something that they could hold, something that reminded them of Tabitha, who was now gone but whose memory they desperately clutched.

This is a very normal thing, and it happens all the time. Whenever pastors or bereavement ministers gather with a family at the time of a death, they often experience what Peter experienced in the home of Tabitha.

Those in grief place in our care the life of someone they love. It's as if they say, "This was our grandmother's (or our father's or our teenager's) life. Consider the intricate patterns; look at the beautiful design. Observe how carefully and lovingly she stitched together the pieces of her life: her dedication to her tasks, her devotion to her faith, her love of her family…all these aspects of her life. See how well she fit them together."

Then they look at us and ask that we help them place the beautiful quilt of that person's life in the hands of Christ.

Silence

There's a little known detail that appears in the opening chapters of the book of Job. When Job's friends gather at his house to console him, they said nothing:

> They sat with him on the ground seven days and seven nights, and no one spoke a word to him, for they saw that his suffering was very great. (Job 2:13)

Some biblical commentators suggest that, in those days, no one had permission to speak to a grieving person until that individual spoke first.

For seven days Job sat in the presence of his friends and opened not his mouth. Once he did, his friends chimed in. The result was something like a pep talk delivered by pessimists.

The conventional theology of his friends gave Job more misery than comfort. How did this happen? Their mistake was a paltry effort to *explain* Job's suffering as opposed to entering into it.

Whenever a death occurs in my parish, I call to mind both Tabitha's quilts and Job's hapless friends. My task and that of the parish bereavement ministers is to be of the need for silence as well as to imitate the graciousness of Peter as he received into his hands the beautiful garments that Tabitha had sewn.

This chapter is about silence, empathy, and reverent observation.

Eulogy vs. the Paschal Mystery

Christ offered his life on the wood of the cross for the salvation of the world. *By his bruises,* in the words of Isaiah 53:5, *we are healed.* The Catholic Rite of Funerals rightly requires that the redemptive sacrifice of Christ be the central point of every funeral homily. Yet many members of bereaved families yearn for some personal references in the funeral homily. Are the two expectations mutually exclusive?

Not at all. John the Apostle tells us that God is love. Therefore, illustrations of human love, when presented in a proper way, are illustrations of God. This is particularly true when the love being described contains the qualities of selflessness contained in the level of love the Greeks referred to as *agape,* that highest form of love, which counts no cost: a firefighter who enters a burning building to rescue people trapped inside, a mother who puts her life at risk to push a child out of the path of a speeding car, or a sergeant on patrol who throws himself on top of an enemy grenade hurled into the midst of his platoon.

It is precisely in this sort of self-giving love that Christians have long seen a reflection of Christ's love for the people He redeemed. Few of us ever attain the heroism of actually laying down our life for the sake of another, yet to the extent that we manage some small embodiment of *agape* in the course of our lives, we reflect, however imperfectly, the perfect sacrifice of the Savior whose death resulted in the stone of the tomb being heaved aside and the gates of heaven flung open wide.

A Grandmother's Crucifix

Near the end of her life, my grandmother suffered from what is recognized today as Alzheimer's disease. At the time that she died, the disease had advanced to the point that her world and everything in it had grown completely strange to her and nothing was familiar. She no longer recognized any member of her own family. She recognized no place as her home, nor could she speak any language that anyone understood. She could only mutter phrases in German, the language of her youth.

On the night she lay dying, she was anxious and afraid. Although other people were present and nurses attended to her as best they could, she was, in a sense, completely alone. When the family was called to the nursing facility where my grandmother was dying, my mother thought to bring with her a small wooden crucifix from the bedroom wall at home.

In a world where my grandmother knew nothing else, she recognized the crucifix!

She reached for the cross and held it close to her until she died later that evening.

I am convinced that, despite the ravages of terrible illness, on some deep level, in that part of us that we call the soul, we recognize the power of the Christ's cross because we retain a memory of human love.

When all else fades—health, vigor, productivity, memory, even life itself—love remains. It is our one comfort and our only hope. Love remains.

As a young boy, I was in agony whenever I noticed my grandmother receding further into the dark remoteness of her disease. Yet I also observed another type of love entering our house: the hours that my mother and sisters spent washing my grandmother and feeding her, the difficulty of the decision to remove her from our home for better care in a nursing facility. I can still recall the lack of recognition in her eyes the first time I went to visit her there.

Yet love remained, and I caught a glimpse of its power when my grandmother reached for the crucifix and held it tight on the night that she died. The experience seared me with a knowledge as hot as a branding iron: the cross of Christ stands solid against the suffering of this world.

It is the power of that sacrifice that brings us to that place called heaven, that level of existence beyond our imagining where all is healed and all suffering is set right; where all is love and death is no more than a bad dream.

Where would we be without this hope?

Objects of Love, Tangible Hope

When Tabitha's friends placed some of the garments she had sewn into the hands of Peter, they wept and, at the same time, spoke of Tabitha's life of charity and love for Christ. The garments and the special care that she had invested in the work of her hands helped her friends describe the quality of devotion that apparently infused her entire life: devotion to her work, her friends, the poor, and the Lord. For Peter, the material he now held in his hands was a tangible expression of the Spirit's gifts in the life of a believer who loved deeply and was deeply loved in return.

Indeed, words about love, when properly spoken, are words about God. This is at the heart of all effective preaching.

When I arrived as pastor at St. Al's, the parish already had a highly effective bereavement ministry. With the large number of funerals in our community, I soon grew to appreciate the training and effort that these volunteers brought to the work of ministering to fellow parishioners in times of grief.

Among the services these volunteers provide is assistance in preparing the funeral liturgy. Normally, the preparation meetings take place in the home of one of the family members. This provides an excellent opportunity for sharing cherished memories. Members of our bereavement ministry often find themselves in situations similar to the one that greeted Peter upon entering the home of Tabitha.

The director of the bereavement committee and I soon began to encourage those preparing the funeral liturgies to view the sharing of memories not only as an important part of their healing ministry, but to include it as part of the liturgy preparation itself. Such memories often provide insight into the selection of appropriate readings and hymns. They also provide invaluable insights for the homilist.

A New Form

In order to help the volunteers integrate this additional request into their visits, a new preparation form was devised that included some additional questions. It asked the volunteer, upon entering a house, to notice and inquire about things that could serve the needs of the family in a way similar to the manner in which "Tabitha's quilts" allowed her friends to connect their grief to the gift of Tabitha's life, love, and faith:

- What did friends and family most value about this person?
- Describe the neighborhood, the home, and any items of importance associated with the one who has died.
- How did that person's faith in God manifest itself?

Below are some funeral homily excerpts that illustrate an interweaving of memories from a person's life in Christ with the saving effect of Christ's paschal mystery.

What did you most value about this person?

Memorable qualities often mirror the best in someone's personality. They also provide a window through which to imagine the joy of God.

Do you ever wonder how people like Paul
come to be so good at love and friendship?
Well, if you ask me, they learn how to be friends
by allowing Christ to be a friend to them.
If we were to summarize Paul's life,
we would have to say that he was a friend to many
and a close friend of God.

Remember the special word that Christ used to describe his
    disciples
on the night of the Last Supper?

Remember what it was?
He looked at them and said,
"I no longer call you servants,
rather, you are my friends"(see Jn. 15:15).

Describe the neighborhood, the home, and items of importance associated with the one who has died.

If possible, we ask to meet with the bereaved family in the home of the deceased. There, like Tabitha's blankets, memories are in easy reach. The visit also demonstrates, in a way that words cannot, the willingness of pastoral workers to enter into a place of sorrow and give silent witness to the enduring promises of Christ.

A "Mary garden" is a flower garden planted with flowers
that are named for or somehow associated with the Blessed
   Mother.
There are hundreds of such flowers and herbs:
marigold, rosemary, lily of the valley,
Madonna lily, rose of Sharon…just to name a few.

Bertha had a deep love of Mary and of her Son.
And she loved the flowers named for Our Lady.

Like a blossom in one of Mary's gardens,
she brought love and compassion
to many people in her ninety-one years of life:
caring for children in the Montessori school,
participating in activities at the church,
working with the Red Cross,
bringing food to the shut-ins…

Her life was like a stroll through a Mary garden,
filled, not with flowers, but with faith and service.

How did this person's faith in God manifest itself?

The willingness of individuals and families to discuss matters of personal faith will vary widely. When broaching the subject seems appropriate, the right choices of biblical texts, songs, and homily content become obvious as the conversation unfolds.

There are those individuals
who hold so close to their heart the gift of faith
that the Bible gives them a special name.

They are called Witnesses.

Our friend Ann was such a person.

I don't know if all of you have yet had the opportunity
to read the chapter from the journal that Ann left for us to
    ponder.
She entitled it, "The Good Days of My Life."

When you read this reflection of hers,
it will remind you of the passage we just heard
about the disciples on the way to Emmaus who,
in the midst of confusion, disappointment, and doubt,
suddenly and unexpectedly
caught a glimpse of the risen Lord.

Like those disciples before her,
Ann came to recognize the face of Christ
even in the midst of her struggle with cancer.

Her own words give witness to life in the risen Christ.
A life that, for Ann, has only just begun!

Summary

The preaching that takes place at the time of death illustrates
the importance of silence…the silence in those settings where
sorrow permeates the air and makes the sound of casual words
ring hollow. In such times, logical thinking is hampered and rational
sequences are difficult to follow.

Given all this, it is usually most effective to organize a funeral
homily around an image, symbol, or visual memory. The excerpts
above—Paul's friendship, Bertha's garden, and Ann's journal—
provide something concrete to help the listeners to better grasp
the hope embedded in the salvation of Christ.

Given the debilitation that grief entails—an experience often
described in terms of drowning—it is preferable that preachers
forego the effort of shouting words of encouragement from the
deck. Something more tangible, like a life raft, is more effective.

But what about situations in which the connections are less
obvious, such as when a person's faith was private, hidden, or
nonexistent? What about situations where anger, hurt, or despair
obscure any connection between a person's death and the redemp-
tion accomplished by Christ?

My answer to this is: Deepen your inner silence and sharpen
your observation all the more. Christ longs to reach out to those in
darkness. As ministers of God's Word, we are to enter into those
dark caves and there discover, perhaps hidden beneath smoldering

ashes of resentment or tucked behind boulders of regret, a candle
stub and a piece of flint…some object that will bring a memory of
human love and a ray of hope from the One whose name is Love.

HOMILY: Christmas Lights

Text: John 20:1–12
Occasion: A Funeral

*The following homily, presented in its entirety, is drawn from a situation
full of the darkness mentioned above. They are the words spoken at the
funeral of a woman named Mary who suffered for many years from clinical
depression. Her suicide occurred close to Christmas and at a time when
she was estranged from her family.*

We all know what it is like to sit in a darkened room
with only the light of one candle burning.
We may not experience this very often,
but when we do, we usually focus on that single flame
and find ourselves comforted by the soft glow of candlelight
that illumines the room and enfolds us with a sense of peace.

But, for some of us, there are few candles and no peace;
only rooms full of darkness…
a darkness so deep that it seems to utterly engulf us.

This season of Christmas, so full of light for many,
is particularly dark for others.

It's a time of year, as we all know,
when the houses on our streets are lit with colorful lights.
And inside those houses families gather
to celebrate the birth of Christ.

But there are some of us who find ourselves
wandering streets that are dark and deserted.
Even though there are many houses
where we would be warmly welcomed and received,
we can't seem to locate the address of any such place,
a place we would recognize as home.
And so, we continue to wander inner streets
of loneliness and despair.

In Mary's life, as we are all painfully aware,

there were—for reasons none of us will ever understand—
many rooms that held no candle,
countless streets devoid of Christmas lights twinkling in
merriment
or porch lights shining in anticipation and welcome.

I am sure that each one of us here in this church
would have done anything we could to help Mary find a
candle.

All of you did the best you could to guide her out of the
terrible darkness;
to give her directions to some street where lights shone
bright,
homes were lit with peace, and doors were opened with
love.

It is agonizing, very agonizing, to realize that we were not
able to succeed
in helping Mary find her way to a place of light,
a room where peace could enfold her
and the glow of God's light could calm her, soothe her, and
reassure her.

Try as we might to help her,
Mary seemed intent on looking for something she could
never find.
It was almost as though she were listening for a voice...
straining to hear a word, a certain word,
that could bring her the inner peace for which she longed.

But the world was too loud.
She could never quite catch the word
or hear the voice that would bring her peace.

Nevertheless, in the sorrow we all feel today,
we do know that there was One
who once entered into this dark and confusing world
seeking those whose lives were like dark rooms without
candles,
those whose lives were spent on dark and winding streets.

His name was Jesus, and we call him our Lord.
Over and over, throughout the scriptures,
he is seen touching the hearts of those no one else could
reach:

He is the Good Shepherd who leaves ninety-nine sheep
and goes in search for the one that is lost.
And when the lost one is found,
he heaves it upon his shoulders and joyfully carries it home.

He is the one seated at a well conversing with a woman
whose life is filled with confusion.
As they converse, he responds to her questions
and there, on that deserted street, the woman finds
healing for her soul and loving acceptance of herself.

The gospel also tells of another woman,
weeping in a pool of despair outside an empty tomb
in a garden near Jerusalem.
Although the sun has just risen,
she is in darkness.
She hastens down deserted streets;
the garden is emptier still.

But there, in that deserted place,
she finally hears what she has been longing to hear.

She hears a voice, and at first, she fails to recognize it.

But then the voice speaks her name:

"Mary."

And suddenly, she knows it is the voice of her Lord.
He has found her.

And she, at last, is home.

CHAPTER 4

Ash's Tack Shed

He sits in the pastor's office, arms crossed, legs stretched out in front of him. Next to Ash sits Trish, his fiancée. She is flipping through a hymnal.

"Here's a nice song. Sort of."

She glances at Ash, frustration evident. "It doesn't matter, Father. Any songs will do."

I reach for the hymnal. "Too many decisions for one day. Should we meet again tomorrow?"

I'd flown to Colorado that afternoon and now found myself in an awkward situation. As a friend of Trish's father, I had agreed to officiate at her and Ash's wedding scheduled to take place in just two days. Upon arrival, I discovered that their elderly pastor had taken ill, and no plans had been made for the liturgy. No readings had been chosen, no music selected. Worst of all, Trish and Ash were experiencing a severe case of wedding-planning fatigue.

Ash leans forward and grabs his cowboy hat off the floor. "You two finish this up. I need to feed the horses."

I put the hymnal aside. "Mind if I tag along?"

Ash isn't being rude, just normal. It's hard to carry on a conversation when someone, in this case *yours truly*, is shoving religion down your throat. In my rush to prepare the liturgy, I have overlooked the fact that Ash, a fine young man with a good work ethic, has been raised with no religious background. I should know that a fellow in his boots would prefer eating dirt in a rodeo arena to flipping through pages of church songs and staring at words such as Cana, Corinthians, and Colossians.

"Ash, you still use hard bits? When are you going to switch to snaffles?"

We are in the tack shed, and I am looking at a wall loaded with tack. As a hunting guide, Ash carries a large overhead of horse gear.

"You've been on horseback in the high country. You want your mount dreamin' off up there?"

"Guess not. I wasn't thinking."

This is more than horse talk. Ash and I are getting to know each other. The switch from office to pickup truck broke the ice, and our shared interest in horses is now providing a common lingo.

The previous chapters focused on how we listen; this chapter zeros in on how we talk. More specifically, it will deal with how our vocabulary determines what we see...and what we might overlook.

More than a Headset

At the expense of sounding like a bank commercial, what can a tack shed conversation teach us about preaching? It teaches us that language is more than "audio information." Language not only labels things, it *creates* things. If not for the word *alfalfa* in my vocabulary, for instance, certain strands of hay stacked in the corner of Ash's tack shed would have gone unnoticed. If I had never heard that word, *alfalfa,* chances are that I would not have noticed the distinct texture of alfalfa stems woven in between the dried grass that generally dominates the composition of hay slated for horse use.

In other words, language functions more like a pair of binoculars than a Sony headset. Without certain words in our vocabulary, specific items fail to get noticed. On a practical level, those items fail to exist.

The ramifications for preaching are obvious. The words of scripture, liturgy, and religious instruction act like a grid, heightening some perceptions, screening out others. No wonder Ash opted out of the liturgy preparation session! All those books with all those words—hymns, readings, and orations—were as foreign to him as Swahili. Imagine the culture shock. The confusion would be akin to someone unfamiliar with equine terminology trying to figure out the function of all those items on the wall in Ash's tack shed.

The religious terminology that preachers and pastoral ministers love—grace, eucharist, salvation, mercy, devotion, offering, sacrifice, revelation, nuptial blessing, and the like—will sound about as moving to someone lacking a religious background as bosal, running martingale, quirt, spade bit, tie-down, and the like, will sound to someone who knows nothing about horses.

How disappointing it must be, not only for couples engaged to be married but for listeners in the pew each Sunday, to be treated with bloodless discourse filled with abstract terms: "religious language" that fails to connect "the goodness of the Lord" with the exhilaration of adventure, the passion of love, the fulfillment of duty, or the achievement of a dream.

———————

Ash is a man whose words are straightforward and few. As we linger in the tack shed after the horses are fed, I ask about his work and how he and Trish will handle the periods of extended separation that his life as a hunting guide will impose on their marriage.

He nods to a stack of feed sacks. I sit down.

"If you ask me, if it's easy, it's not love."

"But if you're not home much…"

"Father," he raises his chin. "Let me tell you about *home*."

He takes a seat on a feed barrel. As we talk, I discover that I am in the presence of a passionate young man whose life has been hard, a life in which the bonds of love take on the qualities of steel.

Ash was the oldest child in a home with no father, and he learned to shoulder responsibility at an early age. In the last three years, he has overseen the care of his mother as she fought cancer. He hoped that she would live to be a part of their wedding, but she died six months ago.

For Ash, the word *home* means more than a house, a wife, or a family. He does not articulate his definition in definite terms, but it is clear to me that he has experienced a baptism of pain and that his salvation—his experience of the power of love in the face of death—is at the heart of the love he will vow to Trish.

It will be up to me to supply the words that will help Ash recognize within the coarse weave of his life the strands of Christ's own love.

The next day, I receive some help.

Trish and I are sitting on the porch of her parents' home. We hold cups of coffee in our hands instead of worn hymnals. After easing her anxiety over the details of the liturgy, I ask what I need to know

"So what drew you to Ash?"

"Oh, Father." She smiles, wrapped both her hands around the cup. "He's rugged." She looks up and gazes across the pasture. The jagged line of the San Juan range rises in the distance. "He reminds me of the mountains."

"Do you tell him that?"

"All the time."

I lean back. "I know just the reading for your wedding: *"I lift up my eyes to the mountains, from whence comes my help"* (Ps. 121:1, *author's paraphrase*).

"I've gone up with Ash. Helped him on some hunts."

"He's a good guide?"

"The best." She takes a sip of coffee. "You know, Father, that's where I feel closest to God."

"In the mountains?"

She nods.

"And with Ash?"

She thinks a moment.

"If he reminds you of the mountains," I prod. "And the mountains bring you to God…"

She looks away. Tears have gathered in her eyes.

Heart to Heart

Couples engaged to be married offer preachers—and those who assist preachers in their homiletic task—an excellent opportunity to sharpen their capacity to connecting real life with real faith.

As illustrated in the example of Trish and Ash, the process involves conversations where the language of faith is given a chance to mold perception and heighten awareness of the presence of God, rather than obscure the movement of the Spirit in hearts already aflame with love.

It begins with identifying experiences of the heart, followed by the assignment of appropriate terms.

How does this process unfold? To begin, think of typical conversations in the life of an engaged couple. Whenever I ask a bride or groom, "So, how are things going?" ensuing topics will likely include:

- Guest lists
- Menu items
- Wedding attire
- Frayed nerves
- Finding a place to live
- Arranging time off from work

If the conversation moves beyond "How are things going?" to "How are you doing?" the quality of topics will deepen, but only slightly:

- "Can't wait for the honeymoon."
- "We'll be glad when all this is over."

With some prodding, the conversation might become substantive:

- "My parents think the world of Todd."
- "I can't believe how fortunate I am."
- "We started off as friends. Now we're going to be married!"
- "She has tremendous compassion."
- "I can always depend on him."

These conversational patterns are the same as those that occur in prayer. Whether our partners are human or celestial, the topics of conversation tend to move from topics of immediate concerns (often expressed in tones of anxiety) down to items of long-term significance (often expressed in tones of appreciation).

An essential step in preparing to preach is spending enough time in conversation to discover where signs of God's presence, like strands of alfalfa in bales of hay, might show up. True to the Greek origin of the word *homily* (*homileo,* which means "conversation"), all parties involved in the process—people, preacher, and God—deserve a respectful hearing.

In light of the amazing discoveries that occur in conversations with one another and with God, my usual approach to preparing to preach at a wedding includes teaching the bride and groom—if they are not yet in the habit of doing so—how to pray together as a couple.

In the experience of shared prayer, engaged couples avail themselves a new language through which to express their love for each other. True to the nature of language, the new words and phrases they learn soon engender a deeper awareness of God's presence residing at the heart of their love.

Lesson Plans, Vocabulary Drills

What are some of the words and idioms that Christian couples learn in the process of praying together? In my experience, most engaged couples are keenly aware of the stress of family and societal expectations as the wedding date nears. "Something important" is pressing in on their life, and they are eager for words and labels to help them understand the excitement, stress, and tense conversation it can engender.

When pre-wedding jitters set in, Jesus' phrase at the wedding reception at Cana, "Fill the jars with water" (Jn. 2:7), can cut through the fretful chorus of hand-wringing second-guessers. The phrase invites the couple to see their practical concerns in light of the Lord's practical compassion for a couple in a similar situation. As a pastor, I have found that, for many couples, this simple Bible verse is the first lesson in learning the value of having "a second language" to counter that of the wedding industry and nervous relatives.

The period of marriage preparation provides marriage preparation teams an opportunity to help engaged couples identify God's grace at work in their lives. The process is similar to that of a regular homily preparation group, in which the words of a sacred text heighten the awareness of God's presence in everyday life. In my parish of St. Al's, we make extensive use of two basic grammar resources: the Lectionary and the Rite of Marriage (readings and prayers for the wedding service, respectively).

Wedding jitters is a common conversation topic and an easily accessible area in which to begin the exploration for grace. In cases where the preferred tuxedoes are not available, for instance, or when witness dresses require last-minute altering, Paul's advice to the Colossians about "proper attire"—the virtues of compassion, kindness, humility, meekness, patience, and love (Col. 3:12, 14)— draws [the couples' awareness to deeper realities.

In situations of intense anxiety, unexpected grace is deeply appreciated!

If new words and phrases add a refreshing perspective to the orchestration of ceremonies and receptions, imagine the possibilities when conversations—with the pastoral team and with God— move to the sacramental mysteries of marriage. It has been my experience that nearly all couples are familiar with prayers of petition, such as "Lord, help us not to have undue worry." When they move on to a more meditative level, the ability of religious language to expand their awareness of God's love and blessing increases exponentially. Consider the illuminating power of the phrase from Genesis 1:27, "[I]n the image of God he created them," to heighten a couple's awareness that, indeed, to be in the presence of each other is to gaze upon an image of God.

As conversations deepen between the couple and those who assist them, and as the experience of prayer deepens between the couple and God, the language of faith begins to highlight spiritual aspects of life that would otherwise escape expression and, thereby, go unnoticed.

For example, in the beginning of the marriage preparation process, if the engaged individuals refer to themselves as "friends," they will soon discover new dimensions contained within the term as they engage Jesus' words: "No one has greater love than this, to lay down one's life for one's friends" (Jn. 15:13).

In addition to biblical texts, the words of the liturgy itself adds insight into the sacramental character of their love, as in the nuptial blessing:

> May you be ready to help all who come to you in need. May the poor find you to be generous friends. May daily problems never cause you undue anxiety, but may your hearts always be on the blessings awaiting you in the life of heaven.

Eventually, individuals grow proficient in this language and, often to their surprise, they discover the truth in the axiom: "To speak but one language is to have but one heart."

There is no other way to adequately describe the distance from conversations centered on "I can't wait until all this is over" to times of prayer infused with the words, "I will love you and honor you all the days of my life."

Summary

The preaching that takes place at the Sacrament of Marriage provides an excellent template for preaching on Sunday.

Jesus once spoke of God's mercy as a full measure of grain poured into the fold of a garment. In a similar way, preachers on Sundays, but especially at weddings, strive to point out the abundance of God's mercy streaming through open windows in domestic churches. It arrives in the echo of a basketball pounding the driveway pavement in summer, beneath the sound of the

furnace in the winter, in the silence between the click of the knife
and fork on a plate at the end of the day, in the feel of table linen
and bed linen, in the quiet before dawn as showers are taken and
coffee is made.

All this grace, in good measure, is available in ordinary lives
that are, in reality, signs and sacraments of our salvation in Christ.
This awareness flows from having a second language—a spare
heart acquired through habits of Bible reading, attending Mass and
praying aloud with one's family.

Listen closely. People talk about God all the time. If it's not
immediately obvious, it's only because they're reaching for the words.

HOMILY: Mountain Silence

Texts: The Song of Solomon 2:8–10, 14, 16a; 8:6–7a;
        Matthew 7:21, 24–29;
Occasion: A Wedding

A couple of years ago,
I was on a trip in the high country
with Trish's father, Pete, and some other friends.
We camped one night on a long ridge that overlooks Silver
     Lake.
If any of you have had the pleasure of making that trek,
you know the serene beauty of the place.
You may also know of the existence
of a frontier cabin, or rather, what remains of a cabin,
in a grove of pine trees not far from the shore.

That night, once camp was pitched,
I walked to the grove and inspected what remained of the
     cabin.
Any trace of a wooden structure is gone.
All that remains is a stone fireplace and chimney.
Unlike the logs that once embraced it,
the stonework stands as solid and straight
as the day it was constructed.

The scene reminds me of the passage we just heard
in which Jesus compares the Word of God
to the durability of a stone foundation.

But it also reminds me of something else.
That remnant of a stone hearth
in a remote region of the mountains
is also a silent witness to the beauty of the mountains
and the inner strength one discovers there.

As all of you know,
Ash and Trish love the mountains,
and they hope to make a living in the mountains
as outfitters and guides.
They have the upbringing, the experience,
and the determination to make that dream a reality.

But the dream of sharing one's soul requires something
    more.
It demands more than prayers and Bible reading.
It requires a love of beauty
and a thirst for adventure.

Let's go back, for a moment,
to the stone hearth and chimney
in the pine grove near Silver Lake.

You know, when the moon is heavy
and the night is full of silence,
the site of what remains of that cabin
leads to thoughts about the family that lived there.
Are there any records of the people who once lived there?
What were the names of the children born there?
How hard were their lives?
How deep was their love?
Did accidents take place?
Did a tragedy occur?
What sort of winter storms did they survive?
Who were their friends?
How often were friends able to visit such a remote
    homestead?

The stone remains.
Yet a man and woman need more than rock
to build a homestead in the mountains.

By virtue of its location, the endeavor also involves
the practice of silence and reverence for God.

As most of you know,
there is a magnificent song that enfolds the high country…
a silent song of beauty and strength.
And to catch a strain of that song
is to long to hear it again and again.

Like the hawk is meant to soar and the bobcat is driven to
    hunt,
we human beings are drawn to that which sings of God.

The song is essential to life.
For Trish and Ash, this song will prove as necessary for their
    love
as a rock foundation will be for their house.

They've heard the song,
and the song has led them here.

How do we know this is true?
It is evident in their love
and in the words they use to describe their love.

If you ask Trish what draws her to Ash,
she'll say, "He reminds me of the mountains."

If you ask Ash what he holds most important,
he'll tell that it's a dream of a home and a family
with Trish at the center…
That is what he longs to have with every fiber of his being.

Can you hear the song God is singing to them?

If you listen closely,
you can hear its echo in an ancient book
called the book of Psalms, where
a heart in love with God
responds to the mountain song of the Lord
with one of its own:
"I lift up my eyes to the mountains
from whence comes my help." *(Ps. 121:1, author's paraphrase)*

The song of God takes many forms,
but those who hear the song scented with pine
and chilled by summer snow
hear God speak as no one else.

And the words transform them.

Just one look at the Bible
and it's clear that God's Word
rings with distinct clarity in mountain air.

It was atop Mount Sinai
that God engraved the Commandments into tablets of stone.

At that moment, God's Word thundered and the mountain
trembled.

It was to the hill country of Judah that Mary rushed
to assist Elizabeth in the birth of her child.
Upon her arrival, Mary sang the praises of God,
and at that moment God's Word was heard
in the melodious voice of a lovely girl.

Years later, during a sermon on a mountain,
Jesus' words tumbled down the gentle slopes,
and at that moment the poor became rich
and the pure of heart heard a promise of God.

On the Mount of Olives, Jesus prayed as no man ever
prayed;
and on the hill called Calvary, he gave up his life
for the life of the world.

The Son of God screamed in pain,
and the world would never be the same.

In the clear air of the mountains,
God's Word is as sharp as light.

How will Trish and Ash
hear the mountain song of God?

Recall the words of the first reading,
and you will hear the sound of a gazelle
scrambling across a field of rock
to reach a perch above a cliff…
the air is thin, the sun is bright.

There, surrounded by beauty,
the gazelle's grace, its very posture,
gives worship to God.

That gazelle is the image of the bridegroom,
a symbol of a man we know as Ash,
a man filled with strength and love.
As the gazelle gives honor to God,
so does Ash on the day of his wedding.

And below, in the clefts of the rock,
the dove finds refuge and peace,
and its loveliness gives praise to God.

Beautiful and serene, the dove is the image of this bride,
our friend Trish,
held today in the hand of God
like a dove shaded by vine and sheltered by rock.

Her praise is unlike that of other brides,
for she has gazed upon the splendor of the mountains
and has heard God's love in the voice of her beloved.

Do you hear it…the song of the mountain?
Can you hear the song God is singing to them?

CHAPTER 5

Chris's Studio

Grace. Some days it flows along like a river, mighty but silent. Other days, like a child on a bike, it whisks by in a flash of color. Some days, it bounces with the dull thud of a basketball as neighborhood kids play a game of "horse" in the driveway. Still other days, it's like the shove of a hand that stops you dead in your tracks. Then, for a minute—or maybe an hour—it stares you down, looks you right in the eye. If it had a face, there'd be a wry smile pulling on the lips.

Grace. God's amazing grace.

That's what I experienced on a Saturday morning last winter: an unexpected shove and a teasing smile.

I was in the home of a parishioner named Chris. He and I had just finished a cup of coffee at a dining room table cluttered with schoolbooks and computer monitors.

He took my cup and carried it to the kitchen.

I took in the room. A bench press sat in the corner, and potted plants lined the windowsill. The walls were heavy with family portraits, a first communion banner, and a shelf crowded with winged figurines offering golden volleyballs, golf clubs, and tennis shoes to the gods of athletic endeavors.

Yes, Chris was a father.

He was also an artist, and I had stopped by to view the progress on a painting of Saint Aloysius Gonzaga, the patron saint of youth as well as the patron of our parish and school.

Chris was excited. The painting was nearly finished. I followed as he began clearing a path to his studio upstairs. He lobbed a teddy bear toward the landing.

"Theresa took an outside job. Guess you can tell who's in charge of picking up around here."

I smiled and decided not to mention my envy.

Chris's studio is actually a corner of the upstairs hallway. And that's where it happened: grace reached out, grabbed me by the shoulder, and stared me in the eye.

I love it when God does that.

A painting, six feet tall and filled with vibrant colors, stood in the corner. The image of Saint Aloysius, with a slight smile on his face, peered down from the heavens, surveying below him an expanse of canvas splashed with lively scenes: a girl on a bike and two boys shooting hoops. In one corner, a student sat at a desk doing religion homework; in the other, a ponderous teenager stared into the distance as though searching for some grace to call his own.

And there was more.

On closer inspection, I noticed a bleacher at an athletic field, crowded with parents and grandparents sitting in rapt attention. Then, next to the bleachers, rows of bungalows like the hundreds that line the streets of Bridgetown, the neighborhood our parish calls home.

My gaze returned to the saint in the upper part of the painting. His hands were raised in blessing. It might have been my imagination, but what I thought had been a subtle smile was now a beam.

This chapter is about paintings, portraits, and snapshots.

Framing

So far, we've discussed several ways to elicit insights for preaching. Each chapter has presented a slight shift in perspective. We've considered various ways to listen to friends discuss biblical passages. We've looked at various words that we use when talking about things of God. We've walked the distance from casual observation to the silence of inner prayer.

We'll now consider how scenes from our everyday life—mental snapshots—frame our experience of God's Word and influence our worship of the Trinity.

When Judy and Karen invited me to tour their workplace, the local bureau of Jobs and Human Services, I was impressed by the order and efficiency of the agency. Each floor of the eight-story building was organized according to various functions.

Karen works as an employment counselor, and Judy, her sister, holds a position in the fiscal oversight department.

"It's my job to keep people on their toes," Judy says.

"No wonder Ted's such a good husband."

She laughs. "He tells me to leave my work at the office."

We step off an elevator. A maze of office cubicles spreads out before us. As Karen and Judy proceed to explain the type of work carried out in various areas, I listen and follow along. But my attention is drawn toward the small, often inconspicuous photographs that decorate nearly every workstation and bookshelf.

There are pictures of babies and youngsters in soccer uniforms; photographs of children on seesaws and teenagers at an amusement park; snapshots of grandparents, rowboats, cats, dogs, and hamsters.

By the time we reach Karen's cubicle, I'm expecting a picture of her husband, David, and their children on her desk. I am not disappointed. In Judy's office, I spot a picture of Ryan and Cody, the same shot Ted has taped to the dash of his pickup.

There is no new revelation here. Nearly everyone has pictures of friends and family sitting on the desk at work or tucked somewhere in a wallet. Such pictures remind us of the reasons we go to work day after day.

But here, at the county welfare agency, they seemed to serve another purpose. They represented a desperate hope: the longing for a world where children are safe, households are stable, income is steady…and everyone smiles for a picture.

It is a hope that unites the human family; and when our spiritual instincts are engaged, the pictures we take with us to work remind us that our daily labor does more than provide our daily bread. Directly or indirectly, our work contributes to the establishment of the reign of God in our cities, our country, and our world.

Preachers often use stories to bridge the distance between biblical passages and the contemporary world. Yet sometimes all we need are snapshots…and folks willing to share them.

The way we *frame* our world—concentrating our focus via picture frames, office windows, TV screens, windshields, computer monitors, kitchen windows, and so forth—determines what we tend to notice and what we tend to screen out.

It also determines where we will most likely catch a glimpse of grace…and where it might be overlooked.

Ginny's Candy Shop

The store is called Supreme Nut and Candy. It is not a place to visit on the way to lunch. When I arrived, Ginny was in the back room pouring over a stack of bills and order forms. Unfazed by the fragrance of chocolate, she asked where I wanted to go to eat.

"If you're overstocked, we can eat here."

She shoved a clipboard into a drawer, and I followed her to the front door, averting my eyes from the wide-mouth jars singing my name.

"Ginny, how do you manage to work here during Lent?"

"You get used to it."

Her face looked tired, and I offered to drive.

At the restaurant, she apologized for being preoccupied. We ordered. Then she informed me that one of her favorite customers had a tragedy in her family.

"You heard the news last night? That was Annette's grandson."

"Who?"

"The boy shot on West Eighth." Ginny looked away. "That was Troy. He was trying to break up a fight."

I didn't recall the boy's name, but Ginny often mentioned Annette, an African American woman who never entered the store without talking about Jesus.

And never left without taking Ginny's hand in hers.

"Did the boy survive?"

"He died this morning."

The rest of our conversation that day was subdued. When we returned to the store, a young woman holding a baby on her hip was waiting for Ginny. She had come to deliver an invitation. As Ginny opened the card, I noticed it was an invitation to a wedding.

The two women hugged.

"You'll be sure to come?" The young woman pushed a strand of hair behind her ear. The edge of her sleeve was frayed.

"I wouldn't miss it!" Ginny smiled and hugged her again. The baby started to cry, and the party headed for the door.

When Ginny returned, I asked about the young woman.

"Long story, Father."

"I'll pray for her."

Ginny was already making her way to the back room. "I wouldn't know who has the longer prayer list, Father. You or me."

My bet would be on Ginny.

That evening the paper carried a photograph of Annette's grandson. Later on, as I pray Evening Prayer, I noticed that the psalms spoke of fear. The words conveyed a sense of foreboding as they spoke of enemies lying in wait and lamented the vulnerability of the innocent.

The next psalm pleaded to God to hear the cry of the poor. So I prayed for a boy name Troy and a young woman hoping to marry a good man.

Once again, a visit to a workplace widened the scope of my perception and deepened my prayer. The ministry of the Word, for preachers and listeners, inevitably involves a mirrorlike effect. Just as sacred words highlight moments of grace in our everyday lives, so do scenes from everyday life heighten the power of the words we pray.

A Church with a View

The Church of St. Aloysius Gonzaga in Bridgetown was built in 1962. Its exterior resembles a white, concrete crown (some claim it resembles a space ship). Inside the church, the pews flank the altar in a 360–degree circle. Visitors often find this arrangement disconcerting: "Where's the center aisle?" Sometimes their comments are more theologically nuanced: "It's so distracting to look at other people when I'm trying to pray."

But the parishioners of St. Al's love their church. The round church has influenced their understanding of how Christ is present in their midst. Many parishioners make an effort to greet neighbors and visitors as the assembly gathers. If they notice someone who appears worried or pensive, many parishioners are in the habit of adding that person's need—whatever it might be—to their own list of prayer intentions.

Worshipers at St. Al's, seated in the round, enjoy a panoramic view. If keen to the movement of the Holy Spirit, they have the chance to observe Christ's words affecting the members of his flock each Sunday. Yet the same opportunity exist wherever Christians worship: whenever someone senses the hope of expectant parents who enter the church and search for a pew, notes the weariness on the face of a friend whose father has fallen ill, admires the faith of a neighbor who leads a Bible study, nods to the coach of a daughter's volleyball team, or observes a widower lighting a candle at the shrine of Holy Mary.

As Mass begins, we listen to the readings, then offer the sacrifice. Our hearts fill with gratitude for the family of faith of which we're a part. Like Jacob, we realize that this is truly the house of God; like sojourners with Moses in the desert, we discover water flowing from flinty rock and manna floating on waves of sand.

This is how the Word of God and the liturgy of the church readjusts our focus and frames our visions anew. In a world where images of materialism flash before our eyes at a dizzying speed, a community that prays has an alternate set of images available. The task for today's preaching is to enable believers to examine multiple fields of vision—from snapshots of teenagers at the workplace to the tears of a woman whose grandson is murdered. Its goal is to make believers alert for signs of grace and piercing cries for justice in the world through which we travel to the Kingdom.

Summary

Some pastors view preaching as a tool for teaching the truths of the faith. Surveys of those who listen to preaching, however, indicate that this is a secondary need. Rather than an explanation of doctrine, most believers look to preaching for a validation of the fact that God is real and that life in Christ makes a difference.

These two vantage points—one starting with abstract truth, the other with practical experience—are complementary, not contradictory.

Knowledge of history and theology is good (vantage point 1). But a *good eye* to complement good knowledge (vantage point 2) is also essential.

Communication about the sacred calls for more than theological formulations. It requires the life experience of the faithful in order to be complete. For example:

- A blessing at a fiftieth wedding anniversary turns a poignant moment into a revelation of God's faithfulness.
- Slamming doors and a shouting match become venues for God's mercy in the preaching of the story of the prodigal son.
- The second thoughts of a Marine recruit headed for Iraq bring home Christ's uncompromising words: "Can you drink of the cup of suffering?"
- A nurse who places a unit of O-negative blood in a medical container and apprehends the mystery of Christ's blood given as remedy for sin, begins to see salvation in terms of a transfusion coursing through the arteries of humanity itself,

with its vessels damaged by disease, its tissue torn by senseless violence.

Are not such scenes—these snapshots and portraits drawn from daily life—as clarifying to the minds of believers as the underlying doctrines they represent?

Note that only the first two examples are set within the context of worship. They illustrate the ways in which sacred settings help us place our everyday experiences within frames of religious meaning.

The latter two examples, those of the Marine recruit and the nurse, illustrate how events in our secular life can serve to increase our "depth perception" of the truths we already hold but long to grasp more tightly.

Homiletic preaching, therefore, does not seek everyday examples simply for the purpose of illustrating a theological truth. Rather, it seeks to model a way of viewing life with an eye for the gracious, surprising, and sometimes shocking moments of God's grace.

HOMILY: Saints in the Chute

Text: Exodus: 17:8–13
Occasion: Twenty-ninth Sunday of the Year

I was talking with a woman named Janet earlier this week.
Her son, Terry, runs cross-country,
and she described a recent meet
that featured fifteen hundred runners.

"He reduced his time on the 5K
by a whole minute," she told me.

Janet is proud of her son,
but the conversation soon turned to what it's like
to be a parent "in the chute."

I was unfamiliar with the term,
so she explained that "the chute"
is another name for the last stretch…but with a difference.
It's the place where the parents and friends,
in fact, all the fans—every one of them—
take up positions to cheer the runners on
as they near the finish line.

Janet went on to try and explain
the exhilaration that she feels every time she stands there,
with a bottle of water and towels in hand,
ready to assist the exhausted runners.

"It's different from a football game," she said.
"In a football stadium, you root for a single team.
But at a cross-country meet
you root for every single kid,
no matter what school they represent."

"Sometimes they collapse at your feet," she said.
"And all you want to do is say,
'You made it! You're here! Great going!'"

Her message was clear,
and it's going to help us discover a clear message
in today's readings…
and it won't matter if you happen to prefer
team sports or individual events:
the message applies to both types of sports
as well as to life itself.

And that message is about perseverance.

Now if you ever find yourself moved
by the energy and determination of an athlete,
you can easily grasp the heart of today's passage
from the book of Exodus,
where two priests, Aaron and Hur,
prop up the arms of Moses,
who is exhausted and tired from strenuous prayer.

Imagine the scene:
Moses seated on a rock,
two men on each side helping him,
as it were, to the finish line.
The stakes are high.
Below them, in the valley,
the soldiers of Israel are in pitched battle
for a land to call home.

When was the last time you prayed with similar desperation?
I suspect that all of us here, at some time or other,

have felt our arms tremble and ache as we held them out in
    prayer,
or have felt our hands hurt from the pressure of our fingers
pressing into the backs of our hands as we pleaded with
    God.

A relationship goes sour;
a dream goes unfulfilled;
or someone we love *desperately*
is suffering *terribly,*
despite our earnest and persistent prayers.

Then, on top of all this,
the Evil One worms into our thoughts
and undermines our confidence,
whispering sinister words
that make us doubt the love and power of God.

No matter how well trained we are
no matter how good the "spiritual shape" we're in,
no matter how remarkable our previous experiences
of God's mercy…
our arms grow weak,
and our lungs start sucking air.

We worry that we might not make it.
We worry that our prayers might not be heard.

But that's when the chute comes into view.
This is where we find friends, even strangers,
yelling encouragement
and reaching out to receive us
with towels and water,
smiles, and cheers.

The church has a name for those folks in the chute.
She calls them "saints."
Some of them are in heaven;
some of them are on earth.

And perhaps you failed to realize it
when you entered this church this morning,
but that's where you are…you're a runner coming into the
    chute.

Every Christian knows that there is no such thing
as an "individual event" when it comes to faith:
We need a team;
we need the church;
we need a parish.
That's the reason we show up for practice each weekend.
If you've been on the team for any length of time,
you realize that the training is demanding.
Faith is hard, and the contests can bring us to the point of
   collapse.

But here, in the chute inside this church,
your arms, like those of Moses,
are supported in prayer.
Not by ancient priests named Aaron and Hur,
but by your friends and neighbors here at St. Al's.

PART 2

Homilies That Multitask

CHAPTER 6

Mary Lou's Pantry

"Show me your friends, show me yourself."

Parents use this line in hopes of influencing a daughter's or son's choice of peers. The child might disagree with a parent's assessment, but the truth of the statement is undeniable: It's *really* important who you hang with.

As a kid, I bought that message. As an adult, I learned to invest it. It's the reason I join with parishioners to reflect on scripture in their homes and endeavor to learn about the environments in which they work. My purpose is not to gather tidbits and anecdotes for the Sunday homily. Rather, it is to "hang out"—that is, to meet their friends, learn their talk, and get a new angle on life. It is part of an ongoing effort to take note of signs of grace beneath magnets on refrigerators, observe how the wood of the cross takes the shape of a produce crate on a migrant worker's back, learn how a truck cab turns into a chapel when the lights of home come into view, and experience a thermos of coffee as an occasion for prayer at a bus stop.

Show me your world, show me the state of your soul.

Manna Outreach is a free store located in a poor neighborhood not far from my parish. A woman named Mary Lou directs an energetic cohort of retirees from St. Al's and other churches on Wednesdays and Saturdays. They sort clothes, stock groceries, contact social agencies, and make a church basement a place of welcome for those who don't have much by way of material comfort or security.

It is a privilege—and a workout—to hang with Mary Lou and her friends. Behind the engaging smiles and lighthearted banter among the staff at Manna Outreach exists an efficient operation that distributes eighty-one thousand pounds of food a year to more than eight hundred families. The focus of the work is spiritual, but the actions are precisely programmed: each shelf is numbered, each storeroom organized, every item categorized.

Hours before the guests arrive, assembly lines of volunteers are abuzz consulting inventories, checking lists, and filling bags and boxes according to preset guidelines:

- Bag 1: toothpaste, soap, personal items;
- Bag 2: dry goods, desserts
- Table A: fresh vegetables;
- Table B: bread;
- Guests with yellow cards: thrift shop;
- Guests with blue cards: pantry;
- Guests with red cards: special needs.

The doors open, and the guests arrive. The scene calls to mind the day Jesus blessed the loaves and fishes while the disciples organized the throng into manageable units, arranging the people like flowerbeds on the green hills of Galilee (see Mk. 6:39).

Christ encouraged people with eyes set on the things of heaven to imitate those whose hands are busy with the things of the earth. The ministry at Manna Outreach thrives on efficiency; the volunteers are adept at organizing grace and packing it into bags.

The ministry of preaching is no different: Those who assist in packaging the Word for Sunday must know the weight of the message and how best to ship it.

This chapter is about organization.

Separate Shelves for Separate Sermons

There is more than one kind of preaching. A quick survey of the various settings in which preaching takes place (street corner, on a television program, in a classroom, at church, etc.) indicates the variety available. This chapter will look at different types of preaching and discuss how, like the bags of food at Manna Outreach, different needs require different containers.

I categorize preaching in four basic types: evangelistic, catechetical, theological, and liturgical (or homiletic). Each type of discourse has a specific goal based, in part, on the needs of the listeners and the setting in which it takes place. Likewise, each type of preaching employs certain strategies to accomplish its goal.

The focus of this book is homiletic discourse, the type of preaching that takes place during a worship service. To help us identify the unique purpose and strategies of homiletic preaching, we'll compare its main components with those of the other three types: evangelization, catechesis, and theological argument.

We'll begin by considering how the expectations of the listeners play an important role in determining what sort of preaching takes place.

When my parishioners gather to reflect on the Sunday readings and offer input into the homily, we begin with a discussion about expectations: What do we expect to happen at worship? What do we hope to hear in the readings? What spiritual guidance are we in need of? And finally, how might the homily draw us closer to God and one another?

Meetings of the pastoral council, parish commissions, committees, and so forth commence with expectations that are action oriented or program driven. The purpose of a homily group, on the other hand, is more reflective: to engage in discussion of the scripture in preparation for the community's encounter with the Lord at Sunday worship. The focus of the meetings, therefore, soon turns to matters that delight or trouble the soul.

But it does so in a certain way…one that results in praise and thanksgiving.

Place yourself in the situation of a father whose teenage son's behavior is out of line. The dad might choose to elicit the help of the boy's mother and together confront the boy one evening in the family room. If, however, the misbehavior concerns magazines of a sexual nature, the father might choose to talk to his son in a different setting, such as the workshop.

Why? Because some settings lend themselves to certain topics and styles of language better than others.

The same is true for preaching. The setting where preaching occurs is a factor in the type of preaching that unfolds. A preacher delivers a different style of discourse on a street corner than does a preacher standing in a pulpit inside a cathedral. A minister speaks to a family gathered in a hospital room in a different manner than does a preacher speaks to a classroom of teenagers.

Regardless of the spiritual needs of individual listeners, the setting itself—the physical space and the occasion at hand—will also play a role in shaping the style and substance of whatever communication takes place.

Bottom Shelf: Evangelization

Turn to the Acts of the Apostles, and you'll find premiere examples of evangelistic preaching: sermons that offer salvation to people in search of meaning and purpose. Conversion is the goal of the evangelistic sermon; its primary strategy is personal witness.

An apt symbol for this type of preaching is the soapbox: The evangelist typically "goes out to the highways and byways" and often shouts to get people's attention:

"You, sir! Are you feeling lost?"

Because time is of the essence, the tone is snappy, the content precise:
"You know, Jesus came to seek out the lost!"

Once contact is made and the topic is identified, a strategy is employed:
"I was once in your position. Let me tell you what I endured."

The pitch is thrown:
"Jesus changed my life; he can change yours."

If the listener hears the call to conversion and responds, the discourse has achieved its purpose: a new person accepts a new lens through which to view the world. For the convert, a new sense of meaning arrives through faith. Through the lens of this faith, the new believer begins to assess life in terms of the death and resurrection of Christ.

Second Shelf: Catechesis

Step into a Sunday school classroom, and you will discover a second type of Christian preaching: catechesis. The term comes from the Greek word for teaching. Catechetical preaching has two main components: information and formation. The catechist is both a teacher and a coach, someone who assists fellow believers, be they young or old, in achieving consistency between the gospel they believe and the lives they lead.

Once someone begins viewing life through the lens of the gospel, the believer must refine that lens to fit the unique circumstances of his or her life. The goal of the catechist, in a manner of speaking, is to provide a set of prescription glasses to accurately "read" the gospel and its implications for personal behavior. The preacher's strategy extends beyond that of personal witness to include the witness of the church at large. Therefore, Bible stories, lives of the saints, and contemporary examples of heroic living comprise the bulk of the topics explored in catechetical preaching. Its tone is encouraging. Its approach is that of offering insight and advice based on normative examples of Christian living.

Third Shelf: Theological Argument

Events occur. Issues come up. Complications arise.

And people wonder what to think.

The third type of preaching attempts to respond to the question, What should we think? A tsunami devastates the lives of countless Asian islanders. The news is dominated by a court case involving medical intervention at the end of life.

How do we begin to approach issues such as these?

If catechesis provides the individual believer with a set of prescription glasses to read the gospel and its ramification for personal behavior, theological argument provides the community with a telescope—that is, a specialized lens through which to study a particular topic.

The preacher in this situation is often a specialist (i.e., theologian, doctor, lawyer, therapist, etc.), a fellow believer who assists the community in analyzing a certain question or issue confronting the church. The goal is to provide a logical framework by which the listener can achieve clarity of thought and form a conclusion that corresponds to the teachings of Christ. The primary strategy of this type of preaching is logical argument. Its strategy is similar to that of a debate: logical propositions supported or refuted by evidence. The topics can range from religious doctrine to political issues, such as, "Given the devastation of a tsunami, how do we view the sovereignty of God?" or "Given what we believe, which presidential candidate should we support?"

Inventory: The First Three Shelves

Evangelization

Speaker: Evangelist
Goal: Conversion
Content: Personal witness
Strategy: Personal challenge

Catechesis

> Speaker: Teacher
>   Goal: Right action
> Content: Normative examples
> Strategy: Advice, encouragement

Theological Argument

> Speaker: Specialist
>   Goal: Right thinking
> Content: Propositions, evidence
> Strategy: Logical argumentation

Top Shelf: The Homily

The names Christians give to Sunday worship vary, but the pattern is consistent: the Mass, the Lord's Supper, the Holy Eucharist, or the Divine Liturgy. When Christians gather to celebrate Holy Communion, the structure of the liturgy is usually a two-part affair:

Part 1: The Liturgy of the Word

> Readings
> Discourse

Part 2: The Liturgy of the Eucharist

> Prayers
> Communion Service

Depending on one's denomination, the discourse that follows the readings is referred to as either a sermon or a homily. Some preachers (and laity) view this discourse as a time of instruction. But what if the homily were seen not as a "time out" from worship, but as part and parcel of it? It would demand that the homily be in harmony with its setting. Like a hymn, its language would be more poetic than didactic. It would lead the congregation to savor a moment of contemplation. In short, the homily becomes the "communion service" of the Liturgy of the Word.

So, preachers, save the soapbox for the street corner and keep the personal advice to a minimum. When the community gathers for worship, the primary goal of the homily isn't conversion (that's for evangelization) or correct behavior (that's for catechism class) or right thinking (that's for a lecture hall) rather, it is to engender praise for the one, true God.

If, indeed, the goal of the homily is the worship of Emmanuel, God-in-our-midst, how can pastors and parishioners best achieve its purpose?

The answer: describe those times and places where the grace of God appears.

Yes, it's that easy. This form of preaching transforms the lens, first proffered in evangelization, into a mirror. As the congregation listens to the words of the preacher, the listeners "see" their lives and their world reflected in the words of the homily. This will lead them to an experience of contemplation wherein they will note how closely Christ walks at their side...or how far they must go to catch up with him.

In the first three types of preaching, language functions in a different manner from the way in which it functions in homiletic discourse. Like the words of the liturgy of which it is a part, homiletic language delights in connotation as opposed to denotation; it strives to take the listener to new, unexplored territory; it relishes emotion and atmosphere as opposed to diagrams and propositions; it is more akin to the language of the frontier as opposed to that of the settlements.

Homily

   Speaker: Pastor, pastoral leader
      Goal: Praise and thanksgiving
   Content: Contemporary experience
  Strategy: Description, metaphor, analogy

Summary

All Christian preaching is of Christ and for Christ. Evangelization conveys information. Catechesis offers solid advice. Theological argument provides certitude. In all three types of preaching, the language is clear, the focus is precise. But if the goal of homiletic preaching is to transport the listener to the gate of heaven, the preacher will need the tools of metaphor, allegory, imagery, and poetry to lead listeners through the frontier of that mysterious realm.

Homiletic preaching, ironically, is most "at home" on the "frontier" between heaven and earth. On one hand, it requires a solid grounding in the day-to-day experience; on the other hand, it inspires a deep longing to transcend the ordinary and experience the sacred.

This, and nothing less, is what we expect from preaching that occurs within the context of worship.

HOMILY: Your Life: Poem or Grocery List?

Text: Isaiah 11:1–10
Occasion: First Sunday of Advent, Year A

> When was the last time you picked up a book of poetry? Has
>   it been a while?
> As in, your *entire* life?
>
> I went to a bookstore to buy a Christmas CD this week.
> I wandered through the magazine section, walked past the
>   coffee shop and glanced at the desserts, skirted a section
>   of computer games,
> thumbed through a couple of novels,
> stopped at a table of biographies.
>
> But I don't recall seeing any section on poetry.
> And if I had, I would not have headed off in that direction.
>   Why?
> Well, it's not something that a guy from the west side of
>   Cincinnati would do.
> (In fact, when I told the Saturday Morning Men's Group
> that I might focus on poetry in this week's homily,
> they suggested I go preach at St. Mary's, Hyde Park.)
> Come to think of it, I don't know anyone—
> Westsider or Eastsider,
> man or woman—
> who reads poetry.
>
> If truth be told, a lot of us have neither the time nor the
>   inclination to do much reading…period.
> And when we do,
> it's a book by Danielle Steele or John Grisham…
> something meant to entertain; a diversion,
> a reprieve,
> a *time-out* and a *time-away* from the world as we know it.
>
> That's what we crave in our entertainment, isn't it?
> Be it the books that we read, the movies we watch,
> or the music we listen to.
>
> Poetry, on the other hand,
> draws us deeper into life,
> as opposed to pulling us away.

Not much time for that.
Not much time for beauty.
Not much time for prayer.
Not much time for contemplation.

And this is wrong.
Because without these things
we lose our sense of God.
So why are we living this way? Why are we living lives
    without poetry?

I'm not talking here about reading a book of verse.
Rather, I'm talking about how you view the world around
    you.
I'm talking about seeing the world through the eyes of…
well, someone like the prophet Isaiah, who, by the way,
was also a poet.

The fact that Isaiah was a poet is, I believe,
one of the reasons we read so many of his passages during
    the season of Advent.
We read Isaiah's writings because one day
he looked around at the shabby time in which he lived and
    said,
"You know, someday things are going to be different!"
And he began to speak about the coming of the Lord.
A time when people living in darkness
will be overtaken by the golden sun of a glorious dawn…
a time when all creation will be transformed:
Lions and tigers will become vegetarian!
And snakes will lose their venom.

His poetry sings of a time to come when young boys
will laugh and wrestle with bears
the way they wrestle with their dads on the living room
    floor.

He saw a time when politicians will be kicked out of office
    and nations will be led by the wisdom of children.
Yes, children with the beguiling power to tame wild beasts
and lead everyone, even insurgents and terrorists, on a path
    of peace.

Too good to believe?
Too illogical to fathom?

Not for Isaiah, it wasn't.
Nor is it for anyone today...
anyone with an ear for poetry
and an eye for God.
Take a young girl, for instance,
whose teacher assigns her a poem.
Would the girl know what Isaiah is talking about today?
Yes. Absolutely. No doubt.

If I were to ask all of you right now to write a poem,
where would you start?
What would you write?
Would you sit down at the desk where you pay your bills
and write a few inspiring words about your mortgage?

Or would you, instead, begin by noticing the angle of
    sunlight streaming through the window.
Maybe you'd step out into the backyard,
breathe in the brisk air of winter, and say,
"This is what I cherish...this air, this sun, this place."
Maybe you'd wait for night, when the house is quiet and the
    kids are asleep—a time to stand at a window
and peer into the sky for a shooting star,
then listen for the silence of the planets.
Then, perhaps you would turn from the window
to check on your children and discover on faces nestled amid
    pillows
a type of poetry no words could ever capture.

Then, as you return to bed, you realize
your life is more like a poem than a grocery list,
more like a song than a complaint.

Maybe contemplation like this doesn't happen very often;
but when it does, it's called *grace.*
It's the experience of your faith helping you see
what children see
and what holy prophets see
and *insist* is possible:
a time when God draws near and transforms the world
through the power of God's Word, the faith in our hearts,
and the poetry in our lives.

CHAPTER 7

Martha's Ambulance

It's a Friday evening, and I'm standing on the roof of a hospital in Cincinnati. The roar of a rotator blade pounds the air, and soon a helicopter hovers into view. For a moment, the machine dances above the tarmac like a giant insect, then it touches down. The engine cuts and the propeller slows. A paramedic teams rushes forward. An accident victim is lifted to a gurney and quickly wheeled inside a waiting elevator.

The name of the company is Health Alliance. A parishioner named Martha is one of its nurses. She's invited me to join her on a night shift. The work begins with climbing aboard the helicopter for a refueling flight to a nearby airport.

Martha introduces me to the pilot. He straps me into a five-point harness, and we lift off. The scene is breathtaking. We swoop across wooded hills of the city and glide above downtown skyscrapers. The flight is gentle and smooth, a series of easy arcs and graceful curves as we follow the path of the Ohio River. Below us, the indigo water glints in the setting sun, and suddenly I'm thinking of angels, the river Jordan, and chariots in the air.

I say a prayer for the accident victim and am struck by the incongruity of peace and trauma in such close proximity. As I gaze across the green hills of a beautiful city—a place of love and life, crime and fear, belief and despair—I sense the joy and sorrow of God.

This chapter is about preaching that presents a broad view of life and the human ache for ultimate meaning.

————

Martha is waiting when we return from refueling; the rest of the night will be spent with her and an ambulance crew on the ground. Their duty is to transport patients between hospitals in a mobile intensive care unit. Like the work of the helicopter crew, it is a combination of urgency interspersed with periods of personal reflection.

"I worked six weeks then had to take a month off. Went to Florida." Her name is Jennifer, a young, newly trained emergency medical technician. She and Martha are teamed together this evening, and the three of us are in transit to pick up a two-year-old with appendicitis.

"Rough start?" I ask.

She nods. "My first two runs were children. Both were abused. It was obvious and horrible. My third run was an accident. I had to pronounce two teenagers dead." She glances at Martha. "That's when I switched to inter-hospital transport."

Martha pats her hand. "You're doing fine, Jennifer."

Martha is a mother of three. Before her children were born, she practiced nursing in an emergency room. "Steel yourself. But never forget they're persons, people with families and loved ones."

Through the back windows of the ambulance, an eight-lane highway is full of cars, some of them speeding. Jennifer looks at the traffic, a pensive look on her face.

"What made you want to become an EMT, Jennifer?"

"It's important work." She reaches down and tightens a strap on the empty gurney between us. "And besides, I want my life to matter."

"Don't we all?" Martha adds.

The ambulance is new, well equipped, and surprisingly spacious. Cupboards laden with state-of-the-art medical devices surround us. Before the run, Martha conducted an inventory: drugs, oxygen, syringes, dilators, and so forth. The equipment is expensive.

Martha is right. Everyone's life matters.

Jennifer is also right: each life needs meaning.

Homilies That Multitask

In the tradition of my church, the purpose of preaching is to proclaim God's wonderful works. The unique version of preaching called *the homily* proclaims these wonderful works in the setting of communal worship. For Catholics, this usually includes the celebration of the Eucharist, or Holy Communion.

In a ritual setting, the preacher is a combination of folk poet and community newspaper reporter. Recall the lens analogy from the previous chapter. At worship, preaching becomes a mirror. As the preacher folds the Word into everyday life and contemporary events, the listeners gaze into that mirror and begin to contemplate signs of God's "wonderful works" that would otherwise go unnoticed.

Homiletic preaching achieves its primary objective—an encounter with the Divine Presence—through use of descriptive language and the present tense.

But what if other important concerns arise? What if the community is going through "a dark night of the soul" during which God seems more absent than present? What if the scripture readings for a particular Sunday call believers to repentance and conversion? What if the season is Lent and the listeners come to church expecting a spiritual tune-up? What if the congregation simply seems to be going through a period of malaise?

This could mean that it's time for a revival. If so, room on the parish calendar might be made for some *evangelistic* preaching. This form of preaching has as its main goal conversion or a renewal of commitment.

Evangelistic sermons address those seeking a deeper meaning in life; therefore, the preacher's mode of delivery is one that grabs attention. Primary strategies include stories about personal conversions and a public testimony of commitment to Christ. In Protestant circles, preachers known as evangelists often conclude their sermons with an altar call. In Catholic circles, mission preachers often conclude the renewal program with a communal penance service.

Preachers in both traditions usually deliver highly charged messages that challenge and confront listeners in a manner that the familiar voice of the community's pastor cannot. Jesus himself noted this reality when he said, "A prophet is not heard in his own town or among his own kindred" (Mk. 6:4, author's trans.).

To understand the distinction between these two types of preaching, it helps to compare the experience of Sunday worship with a family dinner. The words spoken at the family table on Sunday (i.e., the Lord's Supper) are obviously different in substance and tone from words spoken in a bedroom hallway when a teenager breaks curfew. Hence, special times such as revivals or parish missions are best suited for evangelistic preaching—that is, preaching directed toward a thorough-going reassessment of what is truly important and necessary in life.

So, does this leave the pastor off the hook when it comes to words of challenge and confrontation? I wish! A committed pastor will always struggle with the flock's need to deepen its commitment to Christ, and spiritual renewal can indeed be the focus of a Sunday homily. The manner in which the issue is addressed in the context of worship, however, will retain a homiletic rather than an evangelistic flavor.

How do I incorporate evangelistic elements into a homiletic approach? Once again, I look to the lives of my listeners for insight and assistance. Consider the events of the Friday evening, related at the beginning of this chapter. My memories of that evening center on the interplay between the beauty of my city, as seen from the air, and the tragic events that occur in its neighborhoods, streets, and highways.

The beauty and awe clearly relate to the experience of worship and the proclamation of "God's wonderful works." The harsh realities connect us more closely to *evangelistic* moments—dramatic scenes that challenge our deepest convictions about life and its ultimate meaning.

The Bible is chock-full of both types of scenes: the shocking and the sublime. A homily with an evangelistic bent will incorporate both elements. The experiences of two young men, Brent and Lee, will illustrate the importance of both perspectives when "talk at the table" turns deadly serious. Brent's experience represents the "awe and reverence" essential to the experience of worship. Lee's experience draws into the region of life's deepest meaning and the consequences of one's commitment to Christ.

The View from the Mountain

Brent is one of the least expressive people I know. He prides himself on being a man's man, a fellow without a sentimental bone in his body.

Needless to say, he's not easy to read. So I'll never forget what I overheard him say when he and I and a group of friends returned from a week riding the Continental Divide on horseback. First, some background.

For five days Brent was quiet as a monk. He usually took a position in line directly behind my packhorse, and occasionally I'd glance back to see if he was still alive.

Brent had shut down. All he did was look out over the vast valleys and snow-covered peaks of the Rocky Mountains, day after day.

Was he mad? Was he out of sorts? Not at all. I had ridden in the high country numerous times and had seen it happen before. His silence was that of a person lost in contemplation.

I know this because, once we got back to Ohio and stepped off the plane, I overheard Brent tell his wife, "Honey, it was so beautiful. It made me cry."

What do his words have to do with worship? They capture the essence of what we all seek through the experiences of preaching, praying, and partaking of Holy Communion.

Christians in the Eastern Churches refer to the Lord's transfiguration atop Mount Tabor as a luminous portent of the gift of the sacraments. For them, an encounter with the Divine Presence shares elements of wonder like that of a trip to a pristine altitude.

It is an easy notion to grasp. If we only breathe traffic fumes and never attempt to escape the pollution of populous regions in order to garner a view from the top of the mountains, our souls will soon wheeze for lack of fresh air and exercise.

But when we allow ourselves to realize the close proximity of God "whenever two or three" are gathered in prayer, when we open the scriptures and review the marvelous works of God, when we allow ourselves to receive the embrace of Christ in the experience of Holy Communion—the experience of worship might well *make us want to cry.* For when we truly enter this type of prayer, our cramped little worlds open wide and our eyes behold vistas of hope and beauty that we never before knew existed.

This is the rich potential of the ritual experience in which homiletic preaching is embedded. Homiletic preaching's main goal is to open the sacred texts as though opening the gates of heaven, urging believers to take in a splendid view of the kingdom of God.

A handy model for homiletic preaching is the table fellowship that existed between Jesus and such folks as Matthew the tax collector and other sinners. At such times, Jesus' words were far from condemnatory. Instead, his stories allowed the listeners to place themselves within arm's reach of the Father.

Does this mean that references to sin and other harsh realities have no place at the table of Christian fellowship? Hardly. You'll recall that during Jesus' last and most important "table fellowship," the consequences of sin and the bloody slaughter of an innocent Lamb were the main topics of conversation.

The View from a Stretcher

Remember how Jesus' friend Mary sat at his feet when he visited her and her sister Martha in their home in the village of Bethany? Remember how Martha complained that her sister Mary had left her to attend to the hospitality? Jesus of course reminded Martha, "Mary has chosen to visit with me. She has chosen the better part and will not be deprived of it" (Lk. 10:42, author's trans.).

Well, about 543 miles from the village of Bethany, there is a young man from my hometown named Lee Wilker. He is a soldier in Iraq, and his job is to conduct daily excursions in a Humvee on the road between Fallujah and Ramadi.

I don't know if Lee has much opportunity to attend Mass these days, but if he does, I strongly suspect that his experience of Christ's presence in Holy Communion is going to be more like the sacrifice of Christ on Calvary than the quiet conversation between Christ and Mary in the house in Bethany.

If you ever had the opportunity to meet Lee, you would get a real good idea of what dedication means. When he was home on leave a few months ago, his parents invited me to join them for dinner. It was wonderful to see Lee and hear his stories that evening. I came away in awe of his courage and with admiration for Lee's love for his country and his hope for the people of Iraq. But clearly, the most vivid memory of that evening was his commitment to his fellow soldiers and his willingness to give his life for them if necessary.

To hear him tell of that would give you a sense of how much the gift of Christ's blood in the Sacrament of the Eucharist is a matter of life and death. In listening to Lee, I received a sense of how Christ's offering of his blood is like an O-negative transfusion, the universal transfusion rushed to his friends in triage.

For it is our faith that there is no medicine as powerful as *His* medicine. When we claim Christ as our Savior, what we mean to say is that Christ is our medic on the battlefield.

And when we are in a crisis, Christ is there with his strength, his courage—his very own blood to restore our life and dress the horrible wounds caused by the shrapnel of hatred, sin, and disease.

In this sense, the offering of the Holy Eucharist is triage for the soul. Yes, there are days when preaching unfolds spectacular mountaintop views, but on other days the view is from a stretcher.

Summary

Homiletic preaching, like evangelistic preaching, can rise to the challenge of rousing listeners to higher levels of commitment to Christ. It does so in its own unique manner: being clear about harsh realities without sacrificing the welcoming quality of "table fellowship" that characterizes the worship setting.

Below is a comparison of common evangelistic strategies paired with the way similar elements might appear in a homiletic mode:

	EVANGELISTIC PREACHING	HOMILETIC PREACHING
CONTENT	Stories of dramatic "turnarounds" in personal experience	Dramatic scenes drawn from life, society, or the world at large
DELIVERY	Language that challenges the listener to accept Christ	Bold words about life and death
CLASH	Call to repentance	Acknowledgment of power of evil
RESOLUTION	Acceptance of Christ as personal Lord and Savior	Acceptance of Christ's love and mercy through Word, Sacrament, and community

Listeners can help preachers identify evangelistic elements for use within homiletic preaching. Their personal experiences of striving to live the gospel "on the front lines," provide the preacher with examples of what sort of commitment is required in secular and sometimes hostile environments.

The work of the preacher can then focus on fashioning a homily with language sharp enough to chisel contrasts between the world as it is and the kingdom that God would have us build.

HOMILY: Christ: High Priest or Medic?

Text: Hebrews 4:14–16
Occasion: Twenty-ninth Sunday in Ordinary Time, Year B

What sort of reaction
do you have to the title: Christ our High Priest?

No doubt we often think of Jesus as a teacher.

Or we think of him as a brother when times are tough.
Or we approach him as a friend when joy and happiness fills
    our hearts.

Jesus is all of these and much more:
Not just teacher, brother, and friend,
but counselor, defender, healer, and physician of the soul.
The shepherd of the church.
We have little difficulty referring to Christ as our King,
the Lord of Heaven and Earth,
the ultimate ruler and judge of the universe to whom we
    shall one day
render an account of our life.

But how often to you think of Jesus as a priest?
What does that mean to you?
Does the modern-day notion of a priest like me cloud the
    issue?
Does the term mean that he is an administrator of some sort?
A person who sits at a desk overseeing a professional staff,
signing payroll checks,
and making sure the roof doesn't leak and the lights are
    turned out in the gym
after everyone goes home?
Is that what a priest does?

In today's world those of some of the things that a priest
    does.
But it is a far cry from what we mean
when the scriptures inform us that
we have in Christ
a great high priest in the heavens
who has been tested in every way
but has, through it all, never buckled at the knees.
And that it is on the shoulders of this individual of
    incredible strength
that all of us, gravely wounded in the battle against the
    powers of destruction and death—
it is on the shoulders of this incredible individual
that we are carried from the field of battle
to safety.

When the scriptures describe Christ as a priest,
don't think of me or any other priest you might know.

Rather, think of a medic on a battlefield.
Or better yet, because it is by the precious blood of Christ
    that we are forgiven our sins,
think of Christ as the medic with O-negative blood, the
    universal donor
giving his own blood in a transfusion to you.

Why? Because when the Bible uses the word *priest,*
it is talking about a situation that involves three things:
blood,
sacrifice,
salvation.
Or in terms that we might use:
blood, safety, and death-defying courage.
And that's why, when it comes to understanding
what the Word of God means
when it calls Christ our High Priest,
the image of a medic on a battlefield
is a lot closer to the truth than
a modern-day priest standing in a pulpit
or sitting in an office.

If this idea conveys what it means for Christ to be our priest,
how does this affect our experience of the Mass?

We all know that the Mass is a sacred meal.
In some religious traditions it is referred to as the Lord's
    Supper.
And we all know that it is done in commemoration of what
    took place
between Jesus and his disciples on the night before he died.
Yet this ritual, like every other symbol—
like every incident portrayed in the Bible—
has layer upon layer of meaning.
And whereas the Mass begins by taking us into the Upper
    Room
where Jesus is celebrating the Passover with his friends,
it very soon pushes us out the door and outside the city
to the hill of Calvary
where thunder is crashing and the earth is shaking
as Christ—our priest, our medic on the battlefield—is
    himself wounded
and gives his life in sacrifice for our own.

The meal, this sacred meal is interrupted
by the wail of sirens.
We are no longer seated at a table with a friend;
we are in triage and we are wounded and feverish,
and the word comes from the field
that our medic is dead.

But eventually someone comes to your cot
and brings you a sip of wine
to calm your fear
and ease your thirst.
And the person whispers to you
that what you have heard is not true.
The medic who managed to carry you to safety is not dead,
but alive.
And because of him, *you* are alive. You are safe.

Whether you are a soldier under fire in Iraq
or a businessman fighting an addiction to pornography
or a woman with a diagnosis of cancer
or a teenager slogging your way through the darkness of
       depression—
when it comes to waging war against vicious enemies,
the love of Christ and the outpouring of his blood on our
       behalf
is what rescues and saves us!

This is what happens at every Mass.
Yes, deep within the spirit of everyone present,
this is what transpires at every Mass.
For, as the Bible tells us,
"We have a great high priest
who has passed through the heavens,
Jesus, the Son of God…
Let us therefore approach the throne of grace with boldness,
so that we may receive mercy
and find grace to help in time of need" (Heb. 4:14, 16)

These words are true—the truest words you will ever hear.
They are the hands of Christ—our priest, our medic—
cleansing the wounds you've taken
and stopping the loss of blood
with the pressure of his grip!

CHAPTER 8

Mrs. Laib's Speech Class

He clenched his jaw. "I can't."

"Yes, you can."

"No, I can't!"

Mrs. Laib leaned back. This was not the reaction she had expected. Luke, the seventh-grader who stood before her, usually craved attention of any sort—his preferred method being classroom disruption.

She glanced down at the book in her hand. It was the perfect excerpt for him to memorize, she thought. The hero was a boy just like Luke, someone who took extraordinary risks and relished every dare.

"Is memorization the problem?" She asked.

Luke stared back. "It's a stupid story."

"But you said you liked it."

"Nobody would be dumb enough to ski behind a car."

"I'm not so sure." Mrs. Laib fought back a smile as several of Luke's recent antics crossed her mind." Just ham it up, Luke. The class will love it. You'll get lots of laughs."

"I'm not doing it!"

We've all experienced scenes like this—teachers coaching students, parents instructing children, pastors cajoling parishioners. And we've known both sides. On the receiving end of instruction, we can chafe and bristle like a student forced to memorize "a stupid story." Whereas, on the other side of the equation, parents, teachers, and preachers can find themselves flummoxed: "Don't they know this is *good* for them?"

Mrs. Laib sighed. "Just take it sentence by sentence, Luke. The more you repeat it, the easier it gets."

"I told you I can't do it."

"Let's try it together."

She opened the book and read a sentence: "'Carl nodded and said softly, 'I'll get in the ditch...'" She glanced up. It appeared as though Luke was listening. "'I'll get in the ditch,' she continued, ' and we'll tie the rope to the back bumper.'"

Luke rolled his eyes.

"Go on," she coaxed. "Repeat the sentence after me, 'Carl nodded...'"

Luke took a breath. "'Carl nodded. And then he...told his friend to get in the ditch."

"'Carl nodded and said softly...'" Mrs. Laib corrected.

Luke scowled and shoved his hands in his pocket. "I'm not doing this."

Can you blame him? Who likes rote memorization? This approach to learning, to the relief of many, is not utilized as often as it once was. Nevertheless, there are subjects that require some measure of it. Still, getting students to commit dates, poems, or multiplication tables to memory is difficult.

Mrs. Laib rubbed her forehead. She knew that if she could just get Luke to memorize a small section of Gary Paulsen's book How Angel Peterson Got His Wings, *he would soar—just like Carl Peterson, the main character in the story.*

Luke has an excellent sense of timing. She had heard his comic inflection and knew his range of pitch. And besides, Luke could draw on his own adventures to enliven this story about a kid taking dares.

"Luke, let's try again. From the top."

Some teachers—and preachers—view their role in terms of "presenting information." They see the listener as responsible for "applying the information."

Unfortunately, the matter is more complicated than this.

If the subject is technical in nature, such as how to fly a plane, this model works. But if the subject matter involves self-knowledge, such as acting or creative writing, the teacher's role expands beyond that of instructor. The job acquires the additional challenge of coaching.

"I know you can do it, Luke."

He looked toward the window.

It was then that she noticed a change in his expression, and she wasn't sure if she liked what she saw. For just a second, his resistance weakened. But in its place was something else, another hurdle.

The boy was scared.

This chapter is about how homilists address fear, resistance, sin, laziness, and other "instances of inconsistency" in the Christian life.

In the previous chapter, we saw how preachers address the search for meaning as a continuing need in the lives of their listeners. Even though believers come to church to worship God and celebrate the presence of Christ in our lives, a preacher will occasionally need to highlight dramatic scenes that stir the soul and bring us-face to-face with Christ, whom we either accept or reject.

This chapter asks us to put ourselves in the shoes of someone like Luke. We've enrolled in a class, now we don't want to do the work—or we suspect that it is beyond our ability.

How does a community of faith respond to members in this situation? Does the community expect the pastor to simply reiterate the laws, the rules, and the regulations of the church?

"Just take it sentence by sentence, Luke. Just keep repeating the words."

This approach doesn't work.

It is this "nose-to-the-grindstone" approach that has given preaching a bad name. Shoving words down someone's throat seldom results in those words reaching the heart. Committing words to memory may be helpful. But it does not guarantee the enlivening of the soul.

The Christian tradition has a special word for the work of "learning the faith by heart." It's called *catechesis,* and after evangelization, it is the next logical step in the spiritual growth of a Christian.

Catechesis is adjusting your behavior to fit the gospel of Christ. On one hand, the job of the catechist is similar to training someone to fly; it involves conveying technical information in a clear and organized way. But the nature of the subject—authentic Christian living—necessarily involves areas of self-knowledge and self-discovery as well. Like the experience of Mrs. Laib's coaxing Luke in speech class, catechesis involves more than the memorization of facts; it entails identification of inner realities that might stand in the way of a lively performance of personal faith.

This is why, on the journey of faith, pastors, catechists, confessors, and spiritual directors are so important. They serve as "personal trainers" for the Christian who is serious about spiritual conditioning. Many churchgoers identify the need for "personal training" as an expectation that they have of their preacher. They come to church hoping to discover ways to address "instances of inconsistency," those times when they find themselves in Luke's situation: stammering their lines and feeling less than enthusiastic about their performance.

Like evangelization, catechesis is a subtle undercurrent in homiletic preaching.

Words That Echo

Preachers and listeners can work together to address this need. Now, if someone considers the homily as a lecture meant to convey technical information about Christian doctrine and behavior, this will seem to be a strange partnership. "What do I have to offer the preacher?" someone might ask. "What do I know about Hebrew, Greek, moral theology, or church doctrine? It's the preacher's job to teach me."

Such a person is confusing the job of the preacher with the work of a scholar.

When it comes to worship, the setting is more like a gymnasium than a classroom and the words of the preacher are more like the words of a coach. And for those who see the preacher as a personal trainer in spiritual conditioning, it's clear that listener input is essential: "Pastor, I don't think my back is going to take lifting that weight you're suggesting I pick up."

Perhaps this is why the origin of the word *catechesis* had something to do with feedback. In its original form, *catechesis* included the notion of verbal give-and-take. Some scholars detect traces of the idea of repetition, like that found in the question and answer format of old-time catechisms. Others suggest that *catechesis* suggested the reverberating sound of an echo, like the sound of wisdom resounding in the deep recesses of the heart.

The most effective catechists, or teachers, of the faith are those who do more than communicate the content of the faith. True catechists do more than encourage others to memorize facts. Rather, they assist fellow believers in living the faith *with all their mind, all their heart, all their soul, and all their strength.*

When pastors and listeners reflect together on the readings for the upcoming Sunday, it's not to figure out ways to inculcate the truths of the faith. It's to discover how those truths resound in the lives of the members of the community, and to render fitting praise for it.

Problem Behavior

In the previous chapters, the value of listener input focused on identifying times and places where God's invisible presence becomes "noticeable."

But there's a part of Luke in all of us, and there are times when we resist going along with the program, times when we'd rather stuff our hands in our pockets and say, "This is stupid!"

At this point, all the information in the Vatican library isn't going to persuade someone to "get with the program." The issue for the preacher is not one of offering more information. Nor is it a matter of offering information in a clearer, more organized manner. It is, instead, a matter of speaking to the source of the resistance.

Whenever a homily reflection group centers on the lack of human compliance to God's will and law, it is easy for the group to turn judgmental. Sentences get filled with words such as "ought" and "should," and most of the language is directed toward nameless, faceless "other people."

What is the result of discussions like this? Well first, the problems discussed never get resolved. Second, the exercise merely confirms the participants' own sense of self-righteousness. In other words, fingers are pointed and backs are scratched. The conclusion? The world is full of problems, but our little corner is neat and tidy. Christ did not die on the cross so that we could live comfortable lives.

To avoid such discussions and the sort of sermons they might engender, leaders need to be willing to adopt a different sort of language, one that highlights the elements of risks and adventure in God's Word. When rightly directed, a homily reflection group can help the preacher identify the intense challenges that faith presents in ordinary life.

It was then that she noticed a change in his expression...the boy was scared.

Language of the Classroom Versus Language of the Trail

When I find myself resistant to God's invitation, whether it is to live more courageously or more faithfully or to serve with greater generosity or commitment, I can cite many reasons for my lousy performance: sloth, lust, anger, pride, envy, and so on. It is from these capital sins that all my other offenses arise.

Some preachers attack these deadly sins with a vengeance in their preaching. I do not. My reason? I am deeply aware that there is something that poisons my relationship with God more than sin: my fear. God forgives my sins. But fear keeps me just beyond God's reach.

This means that, when a scripture passage suggests a homily that focuses on the need for "good behavior," I think of a boy named Luke and try to find the source of the fear. Judgment belongs to God, so I strive not to accuse. In place of accusation, I propose adventure. After all, when the people of Israel followed Moses into the desert only to end up worshiping a golden calf, it was a result of their lack of trust: "If only we had stayed in Egypt. Sure, we were slaves, but at least we had enough to eat!"

No guts, no glory. No adventure, no freedom.

The journey toward God leads us away from comfortable conditions and self-centered ways. To address issues of right behavior through analysis and advice is the work of the catechist, not the preacher. A catechist's preoccupation, after all, is to convey knowledge and sow wisdom within the student. The language of the catechist, therefore, is like that of the classroom teacher: precise, measured, analytical, and gently encouraging.

The pastor's role, on the other hand, is that of a shepherd; and a shepherd's preoccupation is to provide the flock with green pastures and flowing streams. This means traveling, striking camp, pulling up stakes, folding tent canvas, and heading for the frontier. The language used is blunt and rough around the edges; words are meant to pound on the door of the heart like echoes off a canyon wall, invigorating the sojourners with distant sightings of a new land.

Angel Peterson

Carl nodded and said softly, "I'll get in the ditch and we'll tie the rope to the back bumper. You start slow and pick it up to seventy-five miles an hour…"

At the height of his arc the rope snapped tight and snaked him back under the snow, where for two heartbeats he looked for all the world like a gopher. We couldn't see him at all, just this rippling little bulge of snow, and then he burst forth into the open again.

"Stop the car!"

He lay ahead of us in the ditch…"There's life! I saw his hand move."

Carl raised his head and said. "I heard the angels sing."

"What?"

"I said I heard the angels sing…"
After that nobody ever called him anything but Angel Peterson.[1]

Luke's performance won him an award. But the prize was nothing compared to the rapt audience and his classmate's laughs and applause. Mrs. Laib was right. She told him no one would notice that his knees were shaking; besides, those wobbly knees helped him imitate Carl's uncertain movements as he mimicked strapping the skies onto his feet. Making several attempts and falling down in the process made it even funnier.

He hadn't heard the angels sing, not exactly. But the applause at the end was just about as good.

Summary

The road to God's kingdom is scattered with sharp rocks and an occasional fiery serpent or two. It is not a journey for the weak of heart, and there are times when the pilgrim longs to give up and turn back.

When it comes to addressing the struggle for integrity, the homilist can easily employ some of the strategies of the catechist without sacrificing the primary role of leading the congregation to a liturgical encounter with the Lord.

Adopting the mindset of a coach, advisor, or personal trainer need not lead the preacher into delivering heavy-handed harangues during penitential seasons or when the scriptural text is directed toward reassessing one's particular behaviors.

The following homily presents echoes of the story of Lazarus and the rich man on a school playground, a nursing facility, and a city street. The tone at the conclusion is designed to lead listeners to reflect on the need and power of God's mercy.

It is then that the words follow me begin to

HOMILY: They Called Him Lizard *Build an attitude of perseverance.*
Text: Luke 16:19–31
Occasion: Twenty-sixth Sunday in Ordinary Time, Year C

His name wasn't Lazarus. It was Lizard.
At least that's what the other kids called him.
His real name was Eric.
But the kids called him Lizard.

---

[1]From Gary Paulsen, *How Angel Peterson Got His Name: And Other Outrageous Tales about Extreme Sports* (New York: Wendy Lamb Books, 2003).

He was "that kind" of kid.
A little different.
A little awkward.
Thick glasses.
Hair sticking out in different directions.
His voice a little too loud.
His laughter a little too desperate.
His answers in class were often wrong, if not a little "weird."
He was the kind of boy who dies a little bit
every day at recess.

He attended a Catholic school,
so no one treated him too badly.
The playground moms who patrolled the blacktop
with whistles and bandages
were too vigilant to allow anything like that to happen.
No, there weren't any scuffles with Lizard.
He was just ignored.
And in the complicated world of recess,
that was the deepest cut of all—
a cut too deep for any bandage to do much good.

So, there he stood, day after day, at the edge of the suburban
    playground.
And it wasn't just a boy named Eric standing there on the
    asphalt.
It was also Lazarus waiting at the gate.

In today's parable, Jesus makes us stop in our tracks
and notice this beggar covered with tattered clothes and
    sores full of pus.
And though Lazarus is poor, that doesn't seem to be the
    main point of the story.
The main point, as I read it anyway, is the fact that the rich
    man
doesn't even notice Lazarus.

This seems to be the root of the sin that lands the rich man in
    hell.
I say that because there is a very interesting detail in this
    parable.
Out of all the parables that Jesus told,
this is the only one in which one of the characters has a
    name.

Not a single one of the other parables—the prodigal son, the
    good shepherd, the farmer sowing seed, the women
    kneading bread—
none of them includes a personal name.
Except this one.

That's why I say that this parable is not just about the poor.
It's about anyone who gets called Lizard instead of Eric;
it's about everyone who gets overlooked or ignored.
And while this parable has obvious ramifications
on how we go about sharing what God has given us
with those who are less fortunate,
its message, first and foremost,
has to do with "how we see"
as opposed to "how we act."

The past week,
as I reflected on this reading with the adults
who are studying the Catholic faith and who are considering
    joining our community,
a number of individuals pointed out that the rich man, at the
    end of the story,
still "doesn't get it."
The story starts off with Mr. Gucci Shoes
stepping over Lazarus and his swollen legs
at the doorstep of his gated community.
And it ends without a mention of remorse or sadness or
    sorrow
for all of Lazarus' previous pain.

The rich man's sole concern in hell, as it was on earth,
is his own comfort.
Each one of his words is addressed to Abraham.
Lazarus is standing there right at Abraham's side.
And again, the rich man ignores him.
He has more important things on his mind.
And, you might say, that's where you and I enter the story as
    well.

We, too, have other things on our minds.
You don't have to be rich to have
a lot of "other things" on your mind.

You see, this parable is not an indictment on rich athletes
or corporate executives

or rock stars rolling in millions of bucks a year.
It's about all of us who have a hard time
covering mortgage payments,
food,
tuition,
gas,
braces,
and weekly offerings.

It's about us, not about the money we have or the money
    we'd like to have.
It's not about paying bills; it's about paying attention.
It's about noticing those places—
downtown sidewalks,
nursing home corridors,
and suburban playgrounds—
where Lazarus waits to get noticed
and where we all die a little bit inside
if all we do
is walk on by.

CHAPTER 9

Zeke's Son

The Interstate-40 billboard greets me at the Oklahoma line.

Texas: A State of Mind.

On my CD player George Strait is singing a song about drinking in the "the great wide open," and I can't imagine being happier. I'm on vacation and headed to my favorite destination, a small town in the Texas Panhandle called Nazareth.

Can any good come from Nazareth? That's a question Nathaniel asked before he met Jesus. I don't know what he'd have to say about Nazareth, Texas; but for this preacher—who likes horses and whose pastime is breaking colts—Nazareth, Texas, is just this side of heaven: a small community of strong faith, plenty of cattle, and a lot of folks who know how to rope.

When I arrive in town, the pastor welcomes me at the rectory door and hands me the keys.

"The place is all yours, Jim."

His name is Ken. He's a fabulous pastor who works hard. With few priests in the area available for supply, I know he appreciates the chance to get away.

"Any instructions?"

"No one's sick that I know of. No funerals are scheduled." He frowns. Then he smiles. "But I hear Zeke's gathering cows in the morning."

"Super!"

It's Friday evening and I notice cars and pickups parked near the church. "Is the choir practicing?"

"They're waiting to see you."

I help Ken with his bags, shake his hand, and then head for the church. I step inside, and the music coming from the choir loft sounds twangy. I half-expect lyrics about yellow roses and lonesome doves. I touch my hand to the holy water and pause.

The song is simply a local rendition of "Holy God, We Praise Thy Name." I make the Sign of the Cross and realize how much I missed my friends.

I bound up the steps.

Texas: A State of Mind.

The Texas Office of Tourism is savvy. It produces full-color brochures and posters of Padre Island, the Gulf Coast, the Hill Country, the Guadalupe Mountains, oil wells, the Alamo, rodeos, cowboys, canyons, and more. The Republic of Texas has a wealth of cultures, foods, and regions to offer the visitor, and its Office of Tourism does an excellent job of promoting them all.

But I have yet to see a brochure touting "Texas' Theology-oriented Topology."

Huh?

Think about it. With white sand deserts, fierce landscapes, and vast regions of arid emptiness, Texas offers excellent space for serious prayer.

No wonder it's home to a town called Nazareth.

If asked, I'd offer the Office of Tourism another slogan for its billboards.

Texas: A State of Soul.

This chapter is going to deal with slogans—theological slogans.

Ladders of Abstraction

Do you remember the story of Jacob's ladder? He fell asleep one night and had a dream of angels ascending and descending between earth and heaven. When he woke, he declared, "Surely, this is a holy place, the gate of heaven!" So he erected a memorial stone and called the place Bethel, a word meaning "House of God."

This is how theological reflection often begins: a quiet night, stars in the sky, and weird dreams (or some other memorable event). When morning comes—in the case of a dream—you attempt to shake it off. Or if it's truly God speaking, you won't be able to get it off your mind, and you'll be moved to try to make some sense of it all.

Here's the equation: The earth + the sky + troubled sleep = A new day + a new place to pray + a new slogan to ponder.

Bethel: The House of God.

This is the normal path the Bible takes as it tries to communicate the marvelous mystery of God to ordinary human beings. It starts with earthy experiences, such as those of Jacob, and proceeds to develop sophisticated notions about spiritual things including worship, salvation, justification, reconciliation, and so on.

This approach is also the method most people use to grasp spiritual realities: they start with concrete experiences, let's say, the birth of a child. They then draw some conclusion from that experience about the nature of God and the meaning of life such as, "God is *amazing!*" and "Life is *good!*"

This is also the favored approach of most homilists. Most preachers I know start with their feet firmly planted in real life, climb a few steps of the biblical ladder, then bring something of the mystery of God back down to earth.

The key element, of course, is to keep "grounded"—that is, to keep in mind that our job is to convey something of the awesome mystery of God in a comprehensible manner.

As a homilist by trade, I like the feel of dirt beneath my feet.

From the Top Down

But not everyone sees the world, or the mystery of salvation, from the perspective of a homilist. There are other folks in the God business who prefer to work at desks in that skyscraper of a place called the Bureau of Theological Tourism.

And they love slogans, short for abstract theological propositions. Here are a few of their favorites:

- The Eternity of God: No beginning and no end.
- Jesus Christ: True God and true man
- The Holy Trinity: One God in three Persons
- The Holy Eucharist: The true presence of the Body, Blood, Soul, and Divinity of Christ
- The Immaculate Conception: Mary was conceived without sin

As a preacher, I tend to ignore the goods stored on the third shelf in the preacher's study. Most of my preaching centers on tangible things such as biblical stories, personal experiences, and concrete examples. Whenever a purely theological theme presents itself as a topic for a homily, such as Holy Trinity Sunday or the Feast of the Immaculate Conception of Mary, I find myself experiencing theological vertigo. The height unnerves me. I find the high-altitude air thin and hard to breathe. In other words, abstract thinking tires me out.

I'd rather be curled up in a sleeping bag in the valley, camping out beneath the stars with Jacob.

Square Dancing, Line Dancing, and the Texas Two-Step

Of course, an orderly life demands orderly thought. With no plans or ideas, life becomes like a dance where no one knows the steps. And when the dance involves a whole dance floor of people moving together, the need for agreement on how to do the steps increases.

Preaching that focuses on theological propositions fosters underlying community agreement on important issues. Like the caller directing the steps of a square dance, a theological expert directs the thought process of a group of people moving through a complicated issue or engaging in a unified effort.

I grew up in a rural community where square dancing was as common as rain. The thought of having a wedding or a community dance without several sets of square dances never crossed anyone's mind. Why would it? It's great fun. In close-knit communities people put a premium on everyone getting along with one another. Thus, square dancing helps maintain public order, because it's impossible to be mad while square dancing.

Theology works in a similar way. It's a set of ideas that a certain group of people knows well and agrees with. Like the intricate moves of a square dance, it forms a pattern of common movement.

From the first day that Jesus preached on the shore of the Sea of Galilee, the church has been tapping its feet to a lively tune. Sometimes the tune moves us to get up and dance. When that happens, we need to know the steps; and theologians are the ones who map them out.

Sometimes the steps need to be reviewed. Sometimes they need to be altered. But, of necessity, the basic patterns remain in place so harmony is maintained and celebration can break forth.

This is one way that preachers and congregations can understand the practical impact of abstract, theological propositions. A common theology provides agreed upon patterns of thought that enable groups of people to dance together. Or, to put it another way, theological propositions are our "slogans," condensed phrases that summarize the way a group of believers thinks.

When viewed from the perspective of the pew, the doctrines of faith are the great ideas that determine our identity. They also establish a community's patterns of thought and action.

Sometimes the doctrines are formulated in simple, easy-to-remember propositions that serve a community of faith in the same way a slogan comes to identify a region of the country.

The Nazareth Cemetery

The morning is cool, and the handful of weekday Mass-goers leave church and head for home. Except for Gerty. She goes to her car to retrieve a vase of flowers and is now walking toward the cemetery.

Her eighty-five–year-old brother died a few weeks earlier. I catch up with her and ask if I can come along.

She takes me to his grave, and we say a prayer. Then we stand for a while in silence.

The Nazareth cemetery is well kept. It lies atop a small knoll where the wind never seems to rest. The view is an endless stretch of undulating grassland, and it is impossible to go there without thinking of the harsh realities that the early settlers faced as they tried to scratch out a living on an arid plain.

"Lots of stories here, Father."

"I can only imagine."

A gust of wind blows the vase over. I stoop down to reset it.

"Grave stones are about the only things that don't blow away out here."

Gerty's voice is strong, and there's a trace of defiance in her words. I look up and see that she has braced herself against the wind.

"They say you learn to hang on out here." I stand and brush dust from my hand.

"You've got to or you'll blow away."

We turn back. Like most western Texas towns, Nazareth is mostly boarded up. So far, the citizens have managed to retain a school, a post office, one church, one hardware store, one liquor store, and two restaurants that operate on alternating days.

"George tried his hand at a lot of things." Gerty leans on my arm. "Dairy farming. Sugar beets. Then the wells gave out, so he bought a herd of momma cows."

"Sounds like he worked hard."

"You've got to out here." I feel her grip tighten on my forearm. "What did I just tell you?"

I'm confused and look at her.

She smiles and gives my arm another tug. "You work hard. Or you *blow away*."

Gerty didn't realize it, but in just a few words, she had expressed the underlying identity and unifying principle of a small, agricultural community. Like countless small towns across America, Nazareth remains on the map despite seasons of drought, a failing aquifer, uncertainty in the agricultural industry, and changing governmental policy regarding family farms.

Why do the people of Nazareth stay? Why do they keep hanging on? The reasons are many: family and community connections, a sense of history and belonging, the pride that comes from achievement in the face of difficult conditions. If asked, "Why do you believe in Nazareth?" everyone in town would cite one of these underlying reasons without a second thought.

Theology as Identity

The same dynamic is at work in communities of faith. Depending on the community to which you belong, certain statements just "make sense." They may sound odd to outsiders, but members of a community recognize the familiar sound of their theology when they hear it:

Christ is risen from the dead.
(Of course!)

God created the heavens and the earth.
(Obviously.)

We have been forgiven through the blood of the cross.
(Amen to that!)

The "third shelf" in Mary Lou's cupboard from chapter 6 holds provisions that further the nourishment provided by catechesis. Once believers satisfy their need for consistency between their actions and the gospel code of conduct, another yearning develops.

The concern for "right behavior" moves on to a concern for "right understanding." Just as life in a small town in western Texas entails not only hard work but a strong commitment to certain ideas, life in the church requires basic principles that make the effort to live a certain way make sense.

Summary

The challenge of theological preaching is to loosen up a tightly condensed idea and allow it to breathe the air of ordinary experience. Unlike biblical preaching, the references to everyday life tend to be further removed from Jesus' words about yeast in a lump of dough or Paul's frustration over internal rancor in one of his churches.

This means that when a theological issue confronts a community or when a theological topic is the focus of a particular feast or liturgical season, the rhetorical pressure is intense. A pastor and a homily reflection group will need to adjust to the initial sense of vertigo, because even though a doctrine like that of the Holy Trinity can produce a mental form of nosebleed, a community without theological knowledge is like a region without an identifying slogan.

To neglect the "right understanding" of God in the work of preaching is to endanger the long-term cohesiveness of the community.

An effective homilist will engage an essential doctrine most effectively by drawing the listeners' attention to the fact that a certain doctrine is not some invisible, airborne notion; rather, it forms part of the foundation on which the community stands.

Clear theological patterns of thought keep a community "dancing together." The end result of a homily with a theological focus will find the listeners sensing a tug on their arms from someone like Gerty. They'll sense a deep wisdom from the past explaining to them the reasons we live in a certain way—and why it's important to hang on.

HOMILY: God Traded Places

Text: John 1:1–18
Occasion: Christmas Day

> Last year I received a Christmas card from Zeke, a friend of mine in Texas.
> It was one of those cards that features, on its cover, a family picture.

I'm sure you're all familiar with this sort of Christmas
    greeting.
You may have received a card or two like this yourself this
    year.

I appreciate these kinds of cards a lot,
and they tend to stay on my desk long after the other ones
    have been put away.
In fact, the card with Zeke's daughter and his three sons
    ended up
sitting on my bookshelf all year long.

Yet I have to say that when I visited Zeke and his family out
    in Texas
this past summer,
I was amazed at how much the kids had changed in
    appearance.
(And I'm sure I don't need to tell any parents or
    grandparents here
just how fast kids change and grow up.)
But on the day I visited Zeke and his family,
there was one change that I was not expecting to see.

One of Zeke's boys had had an accident last spring.
It happened to Ryan, the eleven–year-old, one day when he
    and his brother
were helping their dad, who is a rancher, load some steers.
Ryan's leg got injured; and though the injury was initially
    minor, there were complications in the healing process,
    and several surgeries
and a skin graft had to be scheduled.

Although I had known of the accident,
I was surprised when Ryan came walking up to me from
    behind his dad's truck,
surprised at just how pronounced of a limp the injury had
    left him with.

Well, I got another card from Zeke and his wife just this past
    week.
It's the same kind of card,
with the same kids lined up in front of the same fireplace
and looking a year older.
Now, let me ask you, just which one of the kids

do you think my eyes went to first?
Why, Ryan, of course.

Now, you can imagine the picture:
It doesn't show anything except a young boy
posing a bit stiffly with his brothers and his sister—
just a normal kid with a sly smile,
a good-looking kid—
who's already shown a lot of ability on the basketball court
and who is also hoping to do as well as his dad in the rodeo
    someday.

Looking at the picture, I hope the same for him.
I don't know if that dream is going to happen for him.
But I do know, looking at that picture, that there is a real tug
    on my heart for that kid.
The one named Ryan, the one with the limp.

So you can see why I have a special appreciation for that
    Christmas card.
But I would not be sharing a sentiment as personal as this
if it were not to help all of us here
have a deeper appreciation of Christmas.
You see, this particular Christmas card
is going to help us realize that the feast we really celebrate
    today is not Christmas;
it's something more.
That picture of Ryan and his siblings
is going to help us recognize that the feast we celebrate is not
    just the birthday of Jesus;
it's something more.
That glossy picture on that ordinary card
is going to help us realize something about a true mystery
    we celebrate
throughout this season of Christmas,
and that is the mystery that goes by a fancy theological term
    called Incarnation.

This doctrine of the Christian faith maintains
that in the person of Jesus of Nazareth,
God, the awesome creator of the universe,
at one point in our measly human history
entered into the material world of space and time
and walked this earth as a human being of flesh and blood.

And encased within the physical chest of Jesus Christ, the
    son of God,
beat a heart, a human heart,
a truly human heart.
A heart that felt a tug, a pull of compassion
for every kid who would ever live named Ryan,
for every kid who would ever live with a limp,
for every kid who would ever live
whose dreams might not come true.

I don't know about you,
but as far as I'm concerned,
to have a God with a heart like that means everything to me.
Do you want to know why?
Because, like *every one of you* here in this church,
I know I can smile and pose for a picture.
And like *all of you,* I can appear normal and happy.
But God knows I have a limp—spiritually speaking, I know
    darn well
that I'm limping my way through life.

In the same way,
God knows that you too have suffered an injury of some sort.
Your own dreams have taken a hit.
You are not the perfect individual you try to be or hope to
    be.
Yet God, our God, looks upon us with heartfelt love.
Do you suppose that God feels toward us
a bit like Zeke and his wife feel toward Ryan?

Let me tell you a little bit about Zeke.
Zeke is a darn good father.
He loves his kids with all his heart.
But you need to know that it was Zeke
who was backing up the truck hitched to the trailer
that ran over his boy.
It was an accident, of course. Zeke had no intention
of putting his son in harm's way.

Put yourself in his shoes for a just a second,
and you know he would give anything—absolutely
    anything—
to put himself in Ryan's place.
Not only there, in that place behind the cattle trailer by the
    gate,

but every time he saw his boy on a gurney being wheeled
    away for yet another surgery.
He would put himself in that boy's place in a heartbeat.
He would put himself in that place.

It's the human thing to do,
and being human is a glorious thing.
But never has it been more glorious
than in this mystery we call the Incarnation,
when God bent over the world
like a parent bending over a child in pain
and wanting to trade places with that child so bad—so bad
    that it happened!
It actually happened!

This is the Incarnation.
This is the Feast of Christmas.
This is what we adore when we look upon the face of Christ:
a love so deep that it feels the tug of every child ever
    conceived
whose dreams do not come true,
a passion so deep that it enters into the deepest longing of
    every mother and father
to rescue and protect their children,
a compassion so overwhelming that it merges with our
    deepest emotions and longings.
God's heart, God's own heart beating in our souls, beating in
    our chests,
becoming one with us so that we might be one with God.

And someday, some wonderful day, when the surgeries are
    over and the pain subsides and the healing takes hold—
    you know what?—
we will find ourselves loving God with the same intensity
that a boy I know named Ryan loves his dad.

That wonderful day in God's good heaven
when pain and death
are reduced to nothing more than a bad dream;
that wonderful day when
the blind shall see,
and the deaf will hear,
and the *lame* will dance.

CHAPTER 10

Father Christian's Village

It was a new world, and its name was Wurupong. Donna had never been anywhere like it before. At the far end of the room a man removed a swath of loose garment from his shoulder and faced east. He lifted the cup of welcome and recited a prayer.

The words were in a language she did not understand and whose name she could not pronounce.

"When he gives you the cup," the mission director whispered, "pour the contents on the ground toward your feet."

She nodded, wishing her hand would stop shaking.

It was the group's first day in rural Ghana. Following a night's stay in the coastal city of Accra, Donna and five other members of St. Aloysius Parish had traveled hours on mud roads, dodging holes and animals, to reach Wurupong, the village of Father Christian.

The prayer continued, and she looked at Mike.

"He's now invoking the ancestors. When this is over, all of you will be considered a part of the village and members of Father Christian's family."

But she hardly knew Father Christian. Until now, he was simply the African priest residing at St. Al's while studying for an advanced degree back in Ohio. Across the room sat Christian's mother, his sisters, their children, and other relatives.

Now they were her relatives?

The praying stopped. The man removed one sandal and placed his foot on the dirt floor. He moved his hand in a circular motion and poured liquid from the cup. He moved toward her, and she took the cup. A feeling of calm swept over her, and her hand did not shake as she tilted the cup toward her feet.

She passed the cup to Mike, then glanced at Christian's family, their faces intent, their eyes welcoming. And an image came to her of Jesus gathered with his disciples in a small house.

She couldn't remember the exact words, but the scene was vivid: "This is my mother," says the Lord. His gesture takes in the entire room. "These are my sisters and brothers. Whoever hears the word of God is mother and brother and sister to me" (see Lk. 8:21).

This chapter is about words that instill a sense of mission. But first, a quick review.

We believe that the Word of God is everywhere: active, transforming, liberating, and healing. It hovered above the waters of chaos at the beginning of the world. Braided into the desert wind, it whispered to Abraham, Hagar, and Sarah. Soon, God's imperative verbs were etched into heavy stone at Sinai; then nouns were shoveled—nouns like burning coal—into the bellies of the prophets. God's lyrics skipped and danced on the strings of David's lyre; in Solomon's poetry love songs nestled beneath the wings of doves roosting in rocky alcoves.

This Word sings out in the world today and reaches a crescendo in the preaching and praise of worship.

The preaching that occurs in worship proclaims the wonders of God and compels listeners to encounter the Divine Presence, a Presence made perceptible to human senses through the interplay of ancient words with sounds like the hum of commuter traffic, the melodies of Sunday hymns, and the squeal of children splashing in an inflatable pool.

Such are the great and small wonders of God: daily wonders as deep as the tone of organ pipes painted in a body shop, as soft as waves slapping the bow of a fishing boat, as shrill as fans rooting for runners at a track meet.

As a pastor and a preacher, I serve as the community's poet, laboring to put grace into words. Homiletic preaching is nothing less than "sacramental speech."

Yet there are times when a homily might "multitask." In addition to engendering an experience of communion, a homily will renew, instruct, or unify its listeners in the process of escorting them up the stairway of worship.

And so the second half of this book has thus far focused on tones occasionally heard just below the "caught-up-in-prayer" surface of homiletic discourse.

Do you recall some of the examples?

For a nurse named Martha, the Word of God cries for conversion with the urgent sound of a siren. In a middle school speech class, it stammers in a boy's effort to gain self-confidence. In western Texas it clarifies basic beliefs that help a community make sense of and endure hardship and adversity.

These underlying tones are evangelization, catechesis, and theological argument. One final consideration remains: exhortation.

In terms of structure, exhortation is simply another version of theological argument.

Theological Argument

1. A proposition is considered.
2. Evidence to back it up is presented.
3. Listeners nod in agreement.

Exhortation

1. An action is considered.
2. Reasons to take action are given.
3. Listeners are motivated to "run with it."

The difference between theological argument and exhortation is the difference between the brain and the feet. In its simplest form, exhortation paints a vision and calls the community to action.

Hard to Sit Still

The homilies I preach are usually set within the celebration of the Eucharist, or what most Catholics call the Mass. This makes motivational speaking problematic. The last thing I want my parishioners to do after the homily is to get up and leave; after all, they haven't eaten yet.

Even when liturgical preaching is not followed by a communion service, too strong an emphasis on action diminishes the contemplative dimensions of the homily. Exhortation—like evangelization, catechesis, and theological argument—remains secondary when the preaching is taking place in church. If the homily is to remain a homily, its main purpose is to elicit praise and engender an encounter with the Spirit of Christ.

So how does a homilist attend to the desire for Christians to unite their efforts and energy in the service of Christ?

By stressing spiritual solidarity as prior to and essential for group action.

Both of these elements play a key role in exhortation; the first is present-oriented, the second is future-oriented. The distinction is important because when Christians gather for worship, *kairos* time trumps *chronos* time. These two Greek words for time differentiate between moments when time seems to stand still *(kairos)* and the continuing push of seconds, minutes, hours, days, and years that pull us into the future *(chronos)*. The first notion of time savors the present, as when lovers kiss. The second notion is more like a child who can't sit still or, as my grandmother would say, a kid with ants in his pants.

Most adults desire worship that is more like a kiss than an itch.

A sense of solidarity is essential to public worship; human connections foster divine connections. From the congregation's sense of spiritual unity, certain actions flow for service in the world. A homilist is certainly free to address and promote those actions at worship. The call to action will fit into the worship experience if a focus on *promotion* doesn't elbow out the focus on *devotion*.

An Offering of Letters

Donna and Barb sat in my study. Each of them held a cup of coffee, and both of them looked tired. They had returned from the mission trip to Ghana earlier that week.

"How'd the pictures turn out?" I asked.

Their faces suddenly look more tired.

Barb chuckled. "I'm still doing laundry."

"Mine are still being developed," Donna added.

I drummed my pencil on a note pad. "I hope you don't mind my asking your help."

"No. I just don't know where to begin." Donna swirled the coffee in her cup.

On the credenza behind me sat a letter from Bread for the World. A manila container beneath the letter held promotional material for a letter-writing campaign. Each year St. Al's parishioners respond in great numbers to the project. They write letters to persuade elected officials to give high priority to the poor in our country and throughout the world.

"I don't know where to begin either." Barb sighed. "Really, Father, how do you describe a life-changing experience?"

"From the heart?"

She smiled and nodded. Donna continued to swirl her coffee, a distant look in her eyes.

"Well," I leaned forward. "We've got the letter-writing campaign this Sunday. Any ideas?"

Donna looked up, a warm look in her eyes. "I know where you should start." She glanced at Barb. "Tell him about the libation ritual at Father Christian's village."

"Oh, Father. It was so moving."

I picked up my pencil. "Did you meet his family?

"More than that," Barb's smile widened.

"What happened?"

Donna sipped her coffee. "They *adopted* us."

Summary

Sometimes small children have a difficult time sitting still during the service. When this happens, the one holding the child often holds some object before the eyes—a toy, a set of car keys, a hymnal—and, momentarily distracted, the child smiles and reaches for the object.

When gathered in the presence of Christ, the church exults at the sight of salvation being placed within its reach. As the arms of a child are held out in urgent desire, so do those gathered at prayer lift up their hearts to God.

A time will come for the listeners to act on the impulse to carry the saving Word out into the world. But for the duration of the service, like a child focused on something bright and attractive, the homilist strives to keep the attention of the listeners focused on the enticing movement of the Spirit.

HOMILY: Statistics, Letters, and a Village in Ghana

Text: Isaiah 58:6–10
Occasion: Fifth Sunday in Ordinary Time, Year A

When was the last time you received a letter?
I'm not talking about instant messenger or e-mail.
I'm talking about a formal letter, a serious letter.

A letter from a daughter in Iraq
saying she's coming home soon.

A letter from a grandmother to a young man in college
with a twenty-dollar bill enclosed.

A letter from a schoolteacher in Ghana,
a friend of Father Christian—
a letter wishing all the best for our parish here in
    Bridgetown,
a letter expressing hope that you might be able to provide
a few boxes of crayons for the children in her village.

Do you ever get letters like this?

Letters that pull on the strings of your heart?

What if God were to write you such a letter?

What might it say?

Dear Dan, Janice, and family,

Just a note to let you know that you're on my mind constantly.
I hold you close to my heart, as you know,
and I want your deepest dreams to come true.

I'm so proud of your family.
I'm so grateful for the praise you offer me.

But, as you can only imagine, I have many things on my mind.

I hope Billy likes his new baseball glove.
And Dan, I know you work hard
for your money and you got a good price on that glove at Wal-Mart.
Just keep in mind, now and then, where that glove came from.
It's on the label. Haiti. I know some of the workers who stitched it.
They live in a village of about six thousand people, and in that
    country,
generally just two taps of water serve a town that size.
The last time I checked, the lousy conditions there
means that one in five infants die.

You might want to think of that, Dan,
the next time you and Billy play pitch.

Janice, I'm glad you like your new job at the radio station.
That morning news shift comes early,

but you do an excellent job—not only on air
but of keeping your family and household together at home.
I'm writing to tell you that their love for you
runs deeper than you know.

Now, about that starting pay. I realize it isn't much,
and I hope your employers come to appreciate your work
and provide you with a fair wage.
If it helps, keep in mind that Taiwanese workers
who assemble radios for export to the U.S.
are earning about twenty-five cents an hour.

Don't get me wrong—they're thankful for their job,
same as you.
As you know, I take great delight in the hum of commerce
and the benefits that flow from human labor and trade.
The creativity just amazes me!
But of course, from my view, it's a family business,
and I hope that good people like you and Dan
help spread the word that everyone needs a fair chance
for a decent life.

Sincerely yours,
Your Father in Heaven.

I don't suppose any of us have received a letter quite like
    that.
And personally, I don't know how I would respond to such a
    letter.

I admit that there would be a twinge of guilt.
I can't tell you how much I take for granted the things in my
    life—
my car, my food, my furniture, my computer, my house,
not to mention the people who work to make those things
    available.

And I'm not sure how I might honor the request
mentioned in this letter.
How might I "spread the word" that everyone deserves a
    fair chance
for a decent life?

Well, here at St. Al's, a lot of us take the opportunity
—once a year—

to write a letter to our senators and representatives
to urge them to work hard toward this end.

After Mass today, we'll again have this opportunity,
and I'm convinced that God is pleased with this effort of ours.
I know it produces very real and concrete results.

But there's more to it.

This exercise of *government by the people* is notable,
but there is more involved in living the gospel
than knowing economic statistics
and sending form letters to Washington.

For us here at St. Al's, it's realizing that
the gold in our wedding rings,
the teak wood furniture in our living rooms,
and the chocolate candy we pass out on Halloween
may well have come from the land of Ghana
and perhaps even from the hands of people we've come to
     know.

At the door of our church today are photographs of Father
     Christian's family.
You'll see the house in the village in Ghana where he grew up;
the church were he celebrated his First Mass;
and photographs of his mother, his nephews,
and his brother, who is the spokesperson for the chief.

You'll see what sort of house shelters the family of a man
who harvests teak lumber from the forest and makes $1.50 a
     day.
You'll get a sense of how a family lives
in a country where gold is extracted from mines and sold in
jewelry shops around the world.

You'll see that life in Father Christian's world is very hard—
and you'll see that economic statistics have human faces,
and those faces are Christian's relatives and neighbors,
and they are our neighbors as well.

We've all come to know and love Father Christian.
He leads us in prayer; he preaches God's words;
he baptizes our children.

We share our lives with him, and he shares his life with us.
Father Christian's world has become a part of our world.
And because of this our love is deeper
and our hearts have grown larger.

This is what happens when we live the good news.
This is what happens when we take the Eucharist to heart.

Conclusion

The cabin is bedded beneath boughs of hickory and oak. An autumn storm has passed, and refracted light ambers the small clearing. A sodden quilt of leaves lies rumpled on the bank of the pond.

It's Sunday evening, and Cincinnati is a hundred miles to the south. I open the cabin door and step inside.

The woods belong to my brother, but the cabin is family property. I come here to unwind. Campfires in the fall. Ice skating in the winter. Bluegill and catfish in the summer.

Peace and quiet on Sunday nights.

I'll fix supper, listen to country music, and then call some friends on the phone. Then I'll light a candle and pray night prayer. I'll fall asleep to the sounds of owls and bullfrogs, a distant train, the snort of a buck.

A breeze stirs, and I set the prayer book aside. Outside, the bent fingers of a Burr oak shake out a splatter of rain, and I'm suddenly in the barn on the farm of my youth. A summer shower has chased my dad, my brothers, and me in from the field. The barn's tin roof clatters. Outside, the protein in the unbaled windrows is getting washed into the ground.

My dad shakes his head; my brothers sulk. I throw my cap on the plank floor in frustration. But my gesture is all show. If truth be known, the sound of rain is as sweet to me as the smell of cut clover. I'm tired of working and I hope the rain lasts the rest of the day—the rest of the week.

As I settle into a pile of chaff for a nap, I study my dirt-dappled arms. I wonder if they'll ever be as strong as my dad's and brothers', knowing it's the work that makes them so.

Thunder rumbles, and I'm suddenly back at the cabin. The flame of the candle lifts and flicks. The stretch of years from that barn to this cabin saddens me. The sadness grows heavier with the years, and my Sabbath rest grows restless. As a boy I learned there's little comfort in a pile of hay. But this itch tonight has nothing to do with chaff sticking to a sweaty back. Rather, it's a nagging sense of weakness—and a youngest son's worry that in his life his back has not sweated enough.

That's why I've written this book. And it's why I have spent my life trying to heft the Word of God to my shoulder like a sack of feed, only to feel as weak as a thin-armed boy.

Such are my thoughts on a Sunday night in middle age in the middle of a woods while listening to the rain.

I'm not a Lutheran, but I like what Friar Martin Luther had to say, and I like to think that we would have gotten along well. He once claimed that if he had known what preaching entailed, he would not have allowed twenty-four horses to pull him into the pulpit.[1] If I read him right, it wasn't the work itself that caused his complaint; it was the hard fact that the work would never be finished, would never be up to grade.

For who can hope to forge the Word of God to fit the world we know?

––––––––––

I have a friend named Mike. He's a welder. The hottest day in the summer finds him wearing a heavy shirt to protect his arms from the sparks. He doesn't complain, merely states it as a fact: "You'd be a fool not to protect yourself."

His work is a parable of blinding light.

I know an emergency room lab technician named Beth. She draws blood from children seated in the laps of anxious parents, athletes vigorous and confident despite their injuries, and victims of honky-tonk fights reeking of sweat and whiskey.

She hurries. Test results are required within fifteen minutes. But sometimes, despite the pressure, she'll gaze through the lens of a microscope and pause a moment, that brief moment when an abnormality reveals itself and she realizes that she is the only one—besides God—who *knows.*

She reports the results, aware that a drop of blood is about to shatter the life of a parent, an athlete, or another lost soul.

It is a terrible knowledge. When she told me about it, I asked how it felt. Her answer: "It's scary, so I pray."

Her words hold the wisdom of a proverb.

––––––––––

[1]Martin Luther, "Sermon on the Twelfth Sunday after Trinity" (2 Cor. 3.4–6) in *Luther's Works,* vol. 51, ed. Helmut T. Lehmann, trans. John W. Doberstein (Philadelphia: Muhlenberg Press, 1959), 222.

I have a cousin who designs ultralight airplanes. When Tony was eighteen, he was paralyzed in a swimming accident. Now he soars above town like Elijah in his chariot.

His life is the story of a miracle.

Such is the permeating, penetrating presence of the Word. It bakes in the heat of the day like yeast in a batch of dough; it colors the wind like clothes on a line. Like lava soap it scours the grime of sin; it gleams like paint on a new car; and it scans the products of our labor like the ruby light of a laser.

This is what I learned as a boy itchy with hay: Christ lives in muscles that ache and chests that heave—and in minds that wander when rain arrives.

So in the end, it is the thirst that keeps us looking for a suitable word, if not the perfect word, to express *the* Word, the one that somehow speaks of God.

A father recently told me that when he and his teenage son need "to talk," they find it easier in the cab of the pickup. "He's a bit shy," the man explained. "I'm not staring at him, and he's not avoiding my eyes. The longer we drive, the more he talks. The more I listen."

Is this not the desire of God, that we dare to speak and strain to hear words that make sense? Beneath the hum of traffic outside the window and despite the knock in the engine, some things get said. Some of it will make sense, and some of it might sound a bit like love.

You know it's not Peter's boat. You know it's not the synagogue in Capernaum or Martha's kitchen on the outskirts of Bethany. It's just the cab of a truck. Or a trip to the mall. Or the smell of diesel at a bus stop.

But God is there. And come Sunday, you're going to recognize that Voice. You've heard it sing in the grind of a winch; you've felt its cadence in the pelt of the rain.

For Further Reading

Chapter 1

Mulligan, Mary Alice, Diane Turner-Sharazz, Dawn Ottoni Wilhelm, and Ronald J. Allen. "Listener's Relationship with the Preacher." In *Believing in Preaching*, 67–90. St. Louis: Chalice Press, 2005.

Pierce, Gregory F. A. *Spirituality @ Work: 10 Ways to Balance Your Life On-the-Job.* Chicago: Loyola Press, 2001.

Chapter 2

McClure, John S., Ronald J. Allen, Dale P. Andrews, L. Susan Bond, Dan P. Moseley, and G. Lee Ramsey, Jr. "Approaches to Interviewing the Congregation." In *Listening to Listeners*, 149–64. St. Louis: Chalice Press, 2004.

Schlafer, David J. *Surviving the Sermon.* Boston: Crowley Press, 1992.

Chapter 3

Thiel, John E. *God, Evil and Innocent Suffering.* New York: Crossroad, 2002.

Chapter 4

Hilkert, Mary Catherine. *Naming Grace.* New York: Continuum Press, 1998.

Chapter 5

Wardlaw, Don M. "Preaching as the Interface of Two Social Worlds." In *Preaching as a Social Act*, edited by Arthur Van Seters, 55–94. Nashville: Abingdon Press, 1988.

Chapter 6

Baumer, Fred. "Toward the Development of Homiletic as a Rhetorical Genre." Ph.D. diss., Northwestern University, 1985.

Mariani, Paul. *God and the Imagination.* Athens: University of Georgia Press, 2002.

Ramshaw, Gail. *Reviving Sacred Speech*. Cleveland: Order of St. Luke, 2000.

Chapter 7

Buttrick, David. *Homiletic: Moves and Structures*. Philadelphia: Fortress Press, 1987.

Chapter 8

Allen, Ronald J. *The Teaching Sermon*. Nashville: Abingdon Press, 1995.

Carroll, John T., and James R. Carroll. *Preaching the Hard Sayings of Jesus*. Peabody, Mass: Hendrickson, 1996.

Chapter 9

Hughes, Robert G., and Robert Kysar. *Preaching Doctrine*. Minneapolis: Augsburg-Fortress Press, 1997.

Chapter 10

Beckmann, David, and Arthur Simon. *Grace at the Table*. Mahwah, N.J.: Paulist Press, 1999.

Burghardt, Walter J., S.J. *Preaching the Just Word*. New Haven, Conn: Yale University Press, 1996.